Created Equal: The Greatest Lie

by

Ashton Gray

Published by

CH∧LET
BOOKS &
MULTIMEDIA

CHALET BOOKS & MULTIMEDIA
www.chaletbooks.com

Specialty Imprint:
OMEN BOOKS
www.omenbooks.com

Printed by CreateSpace

Also by this author:

Watergate: The Hoax

Coming soon: *Stargate: The Hoax*

Other books from our specialty imprint,
Omen Books:

Murder at Wisteria Pines, by Jon Randall

Sentinel Forces: The God Machine, by Myles Thatcher

Notes From the Editors

On Citations

This work was originally prepared for various versions of electronic publication, none of which currently support footnotes, or even endnotes in any meaningful or useful way. Also, this work was written to be readable and understandable by anyone with a thirst for knowledge and understanding, not to satisfy hoity-toity "style" commands handed down from the ivy-covered ivory towers of academia.

Prevailing conventions and mandates for the unwieldy herd of conflicting and often inadequate citation "standards" were developed in the era of manual typewriters or before, and often serve no practical purpose—other than, perhaps, to torture college students more than they already are tortured by crushing tuition and propaganda.

Our primary editorial policy on citations is that the purpose of any citation should be to ease, not complicate, a reader's ability to find and access sources that have been used for pertinent facts.

Our second editorial policy on citations is: To hell with the alphabet-soup so-called "standards" for citations, such as AP, APA, MLA, CMS, AMA, ASA, MHRA, and all their twisted-sister "standards" from institutions such as Oxford, Columbia, or Harvard. None of them are "standards," because if there were a "standard," there would only be one. A dirty little secret that none of them will confess is that no two "professors" anywhere use these "standards" the same way, and most of the "professors" and "experts" who write textbooks for major publishers have no idea how to "properly" style a citation in any of those "standards." (Actual evidence on file from major textbook publishers such as, e.g., Taylor & Francis.)

Our third editorial policy on citations is that citations are not needed for the opinions of "experts" other than the correctly spelled name of the "expert" and some identifiable pointer to the work where that "expert" bloviated. In the era of the internet, any competent student in elementary school can find any such "experts" and all their bloviations in a matter of minutes.

To those ends, we have made every good-faith effort to present, in the text, sensible and adequate acknowledgment of valid sources of pertinent facts so that an interested reader can follow up and check those facts easily. In a few cases, such as with British History Online, we have included their own citations in whatever "style" they presented them (even though we encountered some instances where their information was in error). Otherwise, our citations are focused on relevant information and usability, not on any dictatorial "style."

If you have any difficulty locating a valid source of any fact herein, contact us:

info@chaletbooks.com

We will make every effort to satisfy your search.

On Dates

Historical material in this book crosses periods of history complicated by Old Style and New Style dates. Where that has been an issue, we have done our best to reconcile events in terms of New Style dates, and have presented them that way so they are easy for a lay reader to follow relative to dates currently in common use. History "purists" have plenty of means (and, we hope, time) to compute the Old Style dates if they choose, but we saw no reason to embroil our more casual readers in technicalities.

Table of Contents

Preface

It is inevitable that some denizens of the lowest strata of intellect—and I am not singling out any given professor or news-media talking head—will bleat and wail that this little volume is a full-scale assault on the most sacred and cherished doctrines of leftist, liberal ideology. It is equally inevitable that other denizens of the lowest strata of intellect—and I'm not singling out any given psychiatrist or politician—will howl and moan that it is a full-scale assault on the most sacred and cherished doctrines of rightist, conservative ideology. I know because I've already heard from some people who have come in contact with the manuscript or parts of it.

The reason such a stark dichotomy can exist is because this book assaults only stupidity, ignorance, irrationality, and blind acceptance of dogma that is, in a word, insane—and that brand of dogma exists on "both sides" of the political spectrum. But this work isn't about two-party politics. This book is about the damage inflicted on mankind by fixed ideas—or, as the French so mellifluously put it, *idées fixe*.

This work is about weighing rational thought and actions against irrational thought and actions. This work is about individuals breaking free of the chains of intellectual enslavement that were forged as fixed ideas in centuries past, but that are being shackled right now onto every student in every "school" in the world.

If you love your chains, keep them—but you shouldn't read this book if you want them.

If you believe, though, that mankind still can rise to greater heights, still can reach for greater freedom, still can climb out of the dungeon of dogma and "everybody knows" group-think to stand in the sunlight of greater personal integrity, of greater personal awareness, and of greater responsibility for self and others, then welcome.

From here, the work must speak for itself.

One last introductory note: Anyone who interprets anything in this work as being condemnatory of Thomas Jefferson or any of the Founding Fathers of the United States either has not honestly read the work through, or has badly misunderstood it. I say without equivocation or apology that my sense of respect for Jefferson and the Founding Fathers is boundless. I hold them in high esteem.

They put their lives, fortunes, and sacred honor on the line for the good of mankind, and in doing so created the greatest nation the world had known, dedicated to a star-high purpose: "To form a more perfect Union, establish Justice, insure domestic Tranquility, provide for the common defence, promote the general Welfare, and secure the Blessings of Liberty to ourselves and our Posterity."

Few men have been their equal. And there's the rub.

Their cause, their fight, was against tyranny. If this book is "against" anything, it is against tyranny—but not just political tyranny: a tyranny of thought, a tyranny of fixed ideas.

The greatest tyranny of thought assaulting the world today is summed up in a tyrannical fantasy that ensnared the Founding Fathers: "all men are created equal." Jefferson did not create that mad dogma, nor did any of the Founding Fathers. The rest of this book deals with who did, and the consequences.

On a personal note concerning this manuscript: I have driven my saintly editors, researchers, and proofreaders to bouts of hair-tearing frustration and distraction with a stream of additions, changes, rewrites, and revisions, right up to the last possible hour before scheduled publication. This paragraph, in fact, is one of them. The point is that any and all typos, grammatical errors, repetitious phrases, or any other error of typesetting and publishing are entirely my own fault, not theirs. They are meticulous and professional, but I have pushed them beyond all reasonable boundaries. If you encounter anything at all that is problematic in that regard, please feel free to write to me at this email address:

info@chaletbooks.com

Put it to my attention and they will forward all email to me. I will be very glad to hear from you, and I will do everything I can in my power to reply and put things right.

May you rise to realize your full worth and potential as the uniquely unequaled individual you are. I believe in you.

Ashton Gray

1. The Equality Myth
A Fatuous Fiction

Whether your concept of the origin of the universe is a cosmic explosion, the spoken command of an omnipotent father figure, the dream of a many-armed god, or the promiscuous coagulation of primordial mist, you will search its width and breadth in vain for two things equal to each other.

The heavens have yet to reveal two equal stars. Every planet in the cosmos is different from every other planet. No rock or boulder ever is equal to any other. No two grains of sand match exactly.

Go into a field or lawn and pick a blade of grass; you hold in your hands a unique creation that has no equal anywhere in the world, or in the universe. The very fact that it is in your hands sets it apart, but even before you picked it, it occupied its own space. It pointed in its own direction. It had its own length, veining, coloring, texture, thickness, weight, roots, and arrangement of unique cells that formed the whole, every detail setting it significantly, dramatically apart from every other blade of grass that exists, that ever has existed, or that ever will exist.

From the cosmic to the microscopic, from the macrocosm to the microcosm, from stellar magnitudes down to molecular level and beyond, there is one message that this universe—however it got here—seems relentlessly intent on dictating, displaying, proving, over and over, infinitely: "There shall be no thing equal to any other."

Yet one of the most universal, pervasive, and inescapable beliefs in the world today is that "all men are created equal."

It is in the schools.

It is in the marketplace.

It is in the workplace.

It is in the neighborhood.

It is in the statehouse.

It belongs in the madhouse.

It is a meaningless myth.

It is the greatest lie.

2. The Mystery of the Missing Creator
The Ultimate Whodunit

The worldwide credulous acceptance of the naive notion that "all men are created equal" is largely attributable to the *Declaration of Independence,* written by Thomas Jefferson, and issued by the thirteen young United States of America in 1776 to sever their ties with England. The word "created" in the phrase "all men are created equal" is a powerful, pithy evocation of religious beliefs implying a single author of all creation—some Supreme Being, some god, who allegedly created all men equal. But *who* was this alleged creator?

The presence of that supercharged verb, "created," booby-traps any attempt at rational discussion of this wholly irrational claim that "all men are created equal." No matter how analytic, impartial, secular, or studious such discussion aspires to be, it meets face-to-face with one of the most difficult and embattled issues in mankind's philosophies, religions, politics, and sciences—all of which attempt to embrace it: cosmology, the origins of the universe.

It is inarguable that a "creator" of some sort is being referred to in the fatuous phrase "all men are *created* equal," because it is impossible to have that which is "created" without having a "creator." But what kind of "creator"? The *Declaration of Independence* makes reference in its first sentence to "Nature's God":

> When in the Course of human events, it becomes necessary for one people to dissolve the political bands which have connected them with another, and to assume among the powers of the earth, the separate and equal station to which the Laws of Nature and of **Nature's God** entitle them, a decent

respect to the opinions of mankind requires that they should declare the causes which impel them to the separation.

Who is "Nature's God"? Where did He, She, or It come from? The next sentence refers specifically to mankind's "Creator"—with a capital "C," which convention will be continued for clarity from this point forward:

We hold these truths to be self-evident, that **all men are created equal,** that they are endowed by their **Creator** with certain unalienable Rights, that among these are Life, Liberty and the pursuit of Happiness.

This arbitrary proclamation that "all men are created equal" has become a cultural, societal, and political flood of Biblical proportions that has all but drowned rational thought. The "created equal" dogma is, on its face, an impossible proposition, which any unbiased glance at life proves conclusively, yet it saturates and submerges the daily lives of countless people in nations and cultures the world over—whether those people subscribe to any religion that might have spawned such an illogical idea or not.

So *who* is this alleged "Creator" that is being called "Nature's God"?

Who—or What—Would Have Created All Men Equal?
It is of utmost, primary, ineluctable importance to determine who—or what—this "Creator" is who supposedly would have created all men as "equal."

The inquiry *cannot be confined strictly to religious beliefs* about man's origin, since some portion of "all men" subscribe to no such system of beliefs, and acknowledge no Creator at all. Atheists, agnostics, and every brand of materialist would reject all talk of a divine Creator of the universe—yet many people in those nonreligious or antireligious categories subscribe unquestioningly to the perverse platitude that "all men are created equal." Some of them will get right out into the streets to march and shout and even riot in protest against anyone and anything that won't conform to their strident decree that "all men are created equal." (The irony seems to be lost on them that the rejection of a Creator is, itself, a bit of a problem for the "created

4

equal" doctrine.)

The number of organized theories and beliefs about the origin of the universe is vast, and the variations on those are kaleidoscopic, because each individual has a unique subjective perception and understanding of even the most dogmatically detailed model, so the first question that must be addressed in seeking the source of the assertion that "all men are created equal" is: Can there possibly be a common denominator to such a diverse collection of cosmological convictions, whether religious, nonreligious, or antireligious?

For practical purposes, there is a common denominator, one that is at least as old as the Creation Hymn of the *Rig-Veda* in the East, as old as Aristotle in the West, and as modern as the Big Bang in the unhallowed halls of science: the Prime Mover.

The Prime Mover and the "Equality" Problem
Even the most materialistic or atheistic theories of origins suggest that some force or energy set the universe into being and motion. The current prevailing nonreligious theory is the Big Bang. That isn't to say that belief in the Big Bang theory is antireligious or that it precludes religious beliefs. Some schools of thought seek to reconcile religious and scientific beliefs—not that one kind of belief is always clearly distinguishable from the other. In talking to any extremely materialistic Big-Banger, for instance, it's never very productive to inquire too closely where the material or the catalyst for the conjectural explosion came from, or how it got there—especially since its postulated existence defies all known laws of physics. The mere question can cause extreme angst and florid sputtering among Big Bang disciples.

In fact, materialists got a new god for themselves in the mid-1800s, and that god's name is "Synergy"—the strangely mystical force that somehow causes *physical matter and energy* to come together in ways such that "the whole is greater than the sum of its parts." It was given a more profound name in 1909 by one of their ranks named Lester F. Ward, who dubbed this metaphysical no-see-um as "Cosmic Synergy." This from people who insist that they are "scientists" and "empiricists." Anything at all in the universe that they are unable to explain, they will chalk up to their fervent religion, Synergism, and its omnipotent invisible god, Synergy. It may be the most fanatical religion ever.

On this subject of synergy, an aside: Wikipedia, to its credit, has become an excellent source of sources—if not necessarily a faithful and impartial steward of facts taken from those sources. One of the reasons Wikipedia has become so amusingly, if blatantly, biased in the area of some of the social "sciences" is that it is guarded at all relevant gates by fanatical materialists whose favorite word in describing anything spiritual is "discredited." Like latter-day, if rabid, versions of Cerberus, the many-headed dog guarding the gates of Hell, they often will bark and snarl "discredited" at anything hinting of a spiritual nature to life, or of abilities that might exceed materialistic models of man-as-animal. In most cases, they make sure to snarl that it's been "discredited" by a "consensus" of members of the "scientific community"—a big fictional generality that they've dreamed up to overwhelm any challenger. In light of that, I simply have to quote here—strictly for amusement and entertainment purposes—the very first sentence of the Wikipedia page on "Synergy," as it stands at the moment this is being written (bold emphasis added):

> Synergy is the **creation** of a whole that is greater than the simple sum of its parts.

You well may think I'm joking, and it is very funny, but, yes: Right there as the fourth word in the sentence is "creation"—without, of course, any explanation of what creator created this mystical creation. In case one of the Cerberus-dogs rushes to change it, it's been archived here:

https://web.archive.org/web/20170923214235/https://en.wikipedia.org/wiki/Synergy

If you're ever cornered by one of these fanatical disciples of Synergism, say that you're perfectly happy to accept his claims if he will simply bring you a jar of synergy. You'll be done. (Pro Tip: That also works with any of the psychobabble psychoestablishment "experts." Just ask them to bring you a jar full of ego or superego or id. You'll then be able to enjoy the rest of the party with rational people.)

All religions hold some acceptance, express or implied, of a Prime Mover—whether it is called God, or The One, or The Absolute, or the Monad, or The All, or First Cause, or Synergy, or any other name for the nameless. Many religious beliefs proclaim the existence of one or more deities, physical or metaphysical, who possess sentience, cognizance, and intelligence, and who in some manner—as varied as the mind and myths of man can conceive—brought into being all that we are, and all that we perceive. An exhaustive catalog of such creation beliefs and purported Creators is too exhausting to contemplate, but a brief review is in order, and is necessary, to investigate whether it's possible that all of mankind could have ended up "created equal"—and if so, how it could have happened.

The early Babylonians told of violent creation in *Enûma Elish,* an epic struggle of perishable gods in which the corporeal, if divine, forms and blood of the vanquished became the very material from which the world and mankind are made. If there is any overarching lesson to be taken from the tale, it is one of extreme *inequality* among these gods, warring for domination, without which inequality there would be no world at all or people to populate it.

Ancient Egyptian creation beliefs evolved through complex concepts, from a bootstrapped god, Atum, who created the world through carnal self-gratification, to Ra, born from a blue lotus, to Ptah, an eternal god who spoke the world into being—not unlike the Judeo-Christian god, who appeared on the scene many centuries after Ptah. The idea of "equality" in the history of Egyptian culture is almost laughable. According to Emory University's Michael C. Carlos Museum, ancient Egypt had a social pyramid in addition to its stone pyramids—and the social pyramid was just about as rigid as its physical counterparts:

> Ancient Egyptians believed that the pharaoh was a god. The pharaoh communicated with the gods for the Egyptian people by performing special rituals and ceremonies in the temples.
> **The Social Pyramid** . . . The pharaoh was at the top of a social

pyramid that looked something like this:
   Pharaoh
   Government Officials—Nobles, Priests
   Soldiers
   Scribes
   Merchants
   Artisans
   Farmers
   Slaves and Servants

Seek not to find "equality" in the Egyptian cosmology or cosmogony.

Some creation myths postulate various incarnations—or non-incarnations; it's complicated—of Demiurge (or lowercase *demiurge*), a god born of gods who fashioned the world and living things from imperfect chaotic matter. (As with the Big Bangers and the Wizard of Oz, address is not encouraged to what's behind the curtain—whether the curtain is made of velvet, explosive potential, pre-god gods, or chaotic matter. In Chapter 4, we're going to brazenly pull back that curtain, like an impertinent, tenacious, toothy Toto. But for now ...) No matter where Demiurge shows up, or in which of many forms, there never is any mention of anything resembling "equality."

Ancient Greeks and Romans had densely populated pantheons of gods and goddesses sporting a wide range of ranks and superpowers—not one of whom was even slightly "equal" to any other. At least one Greek philosopher, Plotinus, attempted to reconcile the concept of Demiurge with the Greek hierarchy of gods and goddesses, and the ancient Greek poet Hesiod wrote an epic poem, *Theogony*, that aspired to plot an entire genealogy of the Greek gods and goddesses. Certain it is that no "equality" emerged in the societies of Greece and Rome from their very unequal gods and goddesses, and slavery was a major driving engine of both civilizations.

Other polytheistic lore, such as the Celtic and Norse beliefs, dominated much of ancient Europe, each with its own set of gods, goddesses, and mystical entities. One count puts the number of Norse gods at over 330. They were extremely *unequal* divine creatures.

The polytheistic tribes that inhabited Arabia and the Middle East for centuries had a horde of specialized deities in their pantheons. In fact, there were so many different branches and sub-branches of gods and sub-gods in the Mid-Eastern region that for untold centuries the Kaaba (or Ka'bah or whatever you want to call it) in Mecca was home to 360 idols that the indigenous polytheists worshipped. None of the worshipped gods or goddesses in any of the polytheistic models and myths had any whiff of "equality" in their status, powers, or jurisdictions, and all known polytheistic cultures included slavery as a matter of course. "Equality" be damned.

While the polytheists were proliferating in the deserts east of the Mediterranean, a man from that region named Abraham (a.k.a. Abram, Ibrahim) claimed startling personal visitations and messages from his version of a One and Only *True* God, whose name, supposedly, was "YHWH." The most common pronunciation is "Yahweh," and another name, arguably, is "Jehovah." (Regrettably, there were no witnesses to Abraham's divine visitations. Parenthetically, Abraham's Yahweh seemed awfully similar to the polytheists' high-up god named "El," perhaps in a different robe. Theologians and archeologists have been grinding and churning themselves into a pudding over that possibility ever since, and likely will go right on doing so until the end of time—assuming there is an end of time, another question upon which they grind and churn. For all their academic titles, their framed parchments, their bulging student loans, their grey hair, and their pompous polysyllabic nomenclature, every one of them issues learned declarations that summate to the same: "We just don't know. Could be. Maybe.")

As a result of Abraham's claims of divine discussions with Yahweh, the creation story of Adam and Eve in the Old Testament of the Bible—shared by Judaism and Christianity—pervaded the West so thoroughly that the majority of Western religious doctrine still pivots around belief in Yahweh as the single author of the universe and all life within it—a personified paternalistic Creator with omniscience, omnipotence, omnipresence, and willful creative purpose. Could Yahweh have created all men as "equal"? Stay tuned ...

A long time after Abraham—roughly 2,600 years later, according to some academics who spend their careers disputing each other—a man from Arabia named Mohammed (or Muhammad, or any way you care to spell it) came along and repackaged that same Abrahamic paternalistic Creator of the universe, renaming him "Allah." Mohammed went alone into a cave and came out declaring himself the *Real* One True Prophet of the *Real* One and Only True God. (Regrettably, there were no witnesses. Sound familiar?) Mohammed said that his new, improved version of the *Real* One and Only True God—Allah—had sent a mystical messenger to him in the cave. That mystical messenger of Allah just happened to be the angel Gabriel, who also just happened to be a major messenger of the Judeo-Christian god Yahweh. In all likelihood, Yahweh was actually the polytheist god El in different robes, which would mean that Allah was really El in different robes, too. (Confused yet? Don't feel bad; all the musty academics are, too. If you can corner one long enough, he might even admit it—as long as no one else is within earshot.)

Mohammed made it unmistakably clear that humanity, as created by Allah/Yahweh/El, was anything but "equal." Mohammed decreed, for example, that a man was worth two women. Mohammed also declared that anyone who didn't bow down and accept everything he said was a *kafir*—a disbeliever worthy of hatred, mockery, beheading, annihilation. As scholar and author Dr. Bill Warner has aptly put it:

> *Kafir* is the worst word in the human language. ... A *kafir* is not merely someone who does not agree with Islam, but a *kafir* is evil, disgusting, the lowest form of life. *Kafirs* can be tortured, killed, lied to and cheated ... robbed, murdered ... enslaved, crucified and more.

Farther to the east, religions and philosophies of the Orient also carry tales of deliberate, premeditated creation by a mystical Creator, such as Brahma in Hinduism—but the Hindu caste system shatters any idea of "equality" in that creation as though it were the cosmic egg falling off a wall.

In some Eastern religions, the unmoved mover, or source of creation, has no name or face or robe. Taoism's seminal work, Lao Tzu's *Tao Te Ching*, describes it as the indescribable and unnamable— depending on which of the more than 175 translations you choose to accept. Here are but a few translations of the relevant passages from the first chapter, with translation attribution:

God (the great everlasting infinite First Cause from whom all things in heaven and earth proceed) can neither be defined nor named. For the God which can be defined or named is but the Creator, the Great Mother of all those things of which our senses have cognisance [sic]. —G.G. Alexander, 1895

The Tao which can be expressed in words is not the eternal Tao; the name which can be uttered is not its eternal name. Without a name, it is the Beginning of Heaven and Earth; with a name, it is the Mother of all things. —Lionel Giles, 1904

The Way that can be told of is not an Unvarying Way; The names that can be named are not unvarying names. It was from the Nameless that Heaven and Earth sprang; The named is but the mother that rears the ten thousand creatures, each after its kind. —Arthur Waley, 1934

The Way that can be described is not the absolute Way; the name that can be given is not the absolute name. Nameless it is the source of heaven and earth; named it is the mother of all things. —Sanderson Beck, 1996

The way that can be talked about is not the eternal Way. The name that can be named is not the eternal name. "Nothing" is the name of the origin of heaven and earth. "Being" is the name of "the mother" of all things. —Tien Cong Tran, 2001

An extension of this concept of mystically anonymous origins presents itself in Buddhism. Not concerning itself with a *personified* Prime Mover, or Creator, Buddhist philosophy speaks of a "Beginningless and Endless Cycle" as a pre-existing condition to existence itself.

As long as a thousand years before either Lao Tzu or Gautama Buddha, the Creation Hymn of the *Rig-Veda* spoke in song of a similar nameless origin of the universe:

At first was neither Being nor Nonbeing.
There was not air nor yet sky beyond.
What was wrapping? Where? In whose protection?
Was Water there, unfathomable deep?

There was no death then, nor yet deathlessness;
of night or day there was not any sign.
The One breathed without breath by its own impulse.
Other than that was nothing at all.

It could be said that such inscrutable eternalness as "The One" or

11

"The Way" or the "Beginningless and Endless Cycle" are missing only a beard and robe to join ranks with personified concepts of the infinite Author of all things, given that intelligence and sentience are implicitly inherent—whether named or unnamed—within the infinite itself. Otherwise, those qualities could not possibly manifest in mankind to any degree at all, great or small. And such qualities among human beings are anything but "equal."

To round out this roundup: On the other hemisphere of Earth, Aztecs allegedly believed in a dual god/goddess entity named Ometeotl as the "creator of all creation." Like the Egyptians, the Aztecs built stone pyramids, and like the Egyptians, the Aztecs also had a rigid social pyramid based on anything but "equality." According to the University of Texas at Austin School of Law, Tarleton Law Library, Jamail Center for Legal Research:

> The Aztecs followed a strict social hierarchy in which individuals were identified as nobles (pipiltin), commoners (macehualtin), serfs, or slaves. The noble class consisted of government and military leaders, high-level priests, and lords (tecuhtli). Priests had their own internal class system and were expected to be celibate and to refrain from alcohol. Failure to do so would result in serious punishment or death. The tecuhtli included landowners, judges, and military commanders. Nobles were entitled to receive tribute from commoners in the form of goods, services, and labor. Noble status was passed on through male and female lineages, and only nobles were permitted to display their wealth by wearing decorated capes and jewelry.
>
> The commoner class consisted of farmers, artisans, merchants, and low-level priests. Artisans and traveling merchants enjoyed the greatest amount of wealth and prestige within this class, and had their own self-governing trade guilds. Commoners generally resided in calpulli (also referred to as calpolli), or neighborhood wards, which were led by a single nobleman and a council of commoner elders.
>
> The Aztecs additionally had landless serfs and slaves. Serfs worked land that was owned by nobles and did not live in the calpulli. Individuals became slaves (tlacotin) as a form of punishment for certain crimes or for failure to pay tribute. Prisoners of war who were not used as human sacrifices became slaves.

Finding no trace of "equality" in South American creation lore, we turn toward North America. There, essentially all the indigenous tribes of Native Americans honored some ultimate Creator, such as Akbaatatdia in the religion of the Crow, and Tawa, the sun-spirit

Creator that the Hopi's revered. But none of the beliefs postulated "equality," either intra-tribal or intertribal. It's regrettable to have to report that many of the Native American tribes made slaves of their captives in war, and had pecking orders in their social structures:

> Early settlers spoke of the head chiefs as "kings," and they were not too far wrong. The chiefs had strong authority and were greatly respected. Some, like the true king of the Natchez, were carried on litters and wore special insignia, such as feather cloaks. Their wives might be similarly honored. They were not hereditary, however. A man attained high rank through demonstrating his superior fitness for it. ...
>
> The individual's ancestry, and certain other experiences including unusual achievements, gave him the right to certain insignia, or "crests," such as are carved on the totem or longhouse poles. ... Out of the variety of crests, rights, and prerogatives developed a detailed system of grading; from chiefs; who had a great deal, down through the nobility to the common people, the poorest of whom had no honors or special rights at all. Below them were the slaves.
>
> (From USDA/NRCS document nrcs141p2_023458, "Traditional Social Structures," 2017)

What of the deist God, then? Could *that* be the god who Jefferson claimed was "Nature's God" and the "Creator" of all men as "equal"? It's impossible to answer because the deist God has no more substance or definition than a fog—and in fact considerably less. The entire point of deism is that God hasn't elected to speak to man or make himself known to mankind in any way whatsoever. He's whatever you want Him—or Her, or It—to be. He's whatever you decide He is. He could be the creature from the Black Lagoon or He could be Tinker Bell or the Invisible Man or Mae West or W. C. Fields, if you wanted to decide that—but then, you couldn't, really, because all of those things are known.

Nobody knows. Nobody ever can know. It's all somewhere over in the Black Hole of Divine Mystery that no one ever can be allowed to know—the same Black Hole that Immanuel Kant, the Chinaman of Konigsberg, fell into, dragging all rational philosophical thought with him. (Don't dare ask the blasphemous question of how anyone knows enough about Kant's "unknowable"—or "noumena"—to tell you it exists; your head will explode.) That's why more versions and perversions of deism and deist "gods" have sprung up than polytheists had idols.

There's no record. There's no deist history of creation, or of how it was done, or of when it was done, or of why it was done. There is *certainly* no deist dogma that says a deist God created all men equal. There's not a hint of it anywhere. It's the ultimate no-see-um.

The Decidedly Uncommon Common Denominator

In all cultures, philosophies, religions, and secular models of creation there is a Prime Mover. Whether endowed with personality and sentience, or endowed with mystical and unexplained pre-existence, or endowed with mystically explosive potentiality capable of giving form and substance to all that is perceivable, a Prime Mover—moved, moving, or unmoved, linearly eternal or cyclically eternal, more-or-very-much-less personified—exists in every lasting philosophy or religion known to man, and even in the most pragmatic, materialistic, detached models known to modern science.

The Prime Mover is the prime common denominator.

Given, then, this pinprick of intersection to stand upon, where even the most atheistic can meet the most devout, where deist meets theist, where East indeed meets West, is there any other common denominator at this dense crossroads of endlessly varied paths? Could it be possible? Is there any trait, quality, or characteristic that is *shared* by every religious and secular hypothesis, belief, and model of a Prime Mover, a Prime Force, a Creative Energy, or a Creative Entropy—a Universe Source?

Yes, there is one thing they all have in common: *They each have no equal.*

From Inequality, Spontaneous Equality?

When the universe itself admits of no two things being equal; when its most inviolable law is that two things cannot occupy the same space at the same time, thereby precluding any chance of actual equality ever occurring; when every known concept of a Prime Motive Force, religious or secular, is without equal, nonpareil, sui generis—whence, then, comes the preposterous conceit that "all men are created equal"?

Is there a personified Creator possessed of even a modicum of intelligence who would squander wondrous, infinite creative potential on a mundane, monotonous, homogenized, humdrum class of created thing in which every one of those created things was "created equal"?

Is there some non-sentient creation model where the randomness of explosion or condensation could somehow result in an endless stream of perfect protoplasmic "created equal" clones? (Has any materialist anywhere been bright enough to calculate the odds on that ever happening, or does materialism itself induce terminal doltishness?)

So whodunit? *Who*—or *what*—was Thomas Jefferson referring to with the word "Creator" and the made-up name "Nature's God"?

3. Creating the Creator
A Philosophical Felony of Fallacy

The men who endorsed the *Declaration of Independence* and its "created equal" decree, including Jefferson, were engaged in an attempt to secure and guarantee religious freedom in general, but all of the authors and signers had been involved with, and influenced by, some denomination of Christianity, or, for a few, by deism. The nebulous name "Nature's God" used in the *Declaration of Independence* has some vague echoes of deism, but the phrase does not necessarily *exclude* the Judeo-Christian god Yahweh. Whether the anonymous "Creator" at issue is the Judeo-Christian god has long been an open question. That question needs to be answered and closed once and for all.

Considering, arguendo, that the Abrahamic Judeo-Christian god Yahweh is the "Creator" being credited with—or accused of—creating all men equal, is there any scriptural foundation whatsoever for postulating such a gargantuan lump of creative tedium? Is there anything in the writings of the Old Testament or New Testament—anywhere in all the literature—that says "all men are created equal"?

Surely there is. Surely there is some authority somewhere, *anywhere,* in the Judeo-Christian teachings to substantiate this assertion—fully endorsed by celebrated, lionized, exalted Jewish and Christian men—that some form of cookie-cutter "created equal" man-manufacturing was the pinnacle of this Creator's "creation."

But there isn't.

An exhaustive, meticulous search for an answer found nothing. Nothing even close. It is a dry well.

But it's worse than that: The Judeo-Christian scripture annihilates any such idea of "equality" among men.

For example, there's the following statement that came in a dream to Solomon, attributed to the Judeo-Christian Creator himself, of record at 1 Kings 3:12-13 (emphasis added):

> Behold, I have done according to thy words: lo, I have given thee a wise and an understanding heart; so that **there was none like thee before thee, neither after thee shall any arise like unto thee.**
> And I have also given thee that which thou hast not asked, both riches, and honour: so that **there shall not be any among the kings like unto thee** all thy days. (King James Version)

You read Him right; He said "none like thee," before or since. That's from the version of the Bible that was extant in 1776. A more recent translation puts it this way (bold emphasis added):

> Behold, I have done as you asked. I have given you a wise, discerning mind, so that **no one before you was your equal, nor shall any arise after you equal to you.**
> I have also given you what you have not asked, both riches and honor, so that **there shall not be any among the kings equal to you** all your days. (Amplified Bible, Classic Edition)

No equal. Period. The same Judeo-Christian god is on record as declaring, in Jeremiah 31:34:

> And they shall teach no more every man his neighbour, and every man his brother, saying, Know the Lord: for they shall all know me, **from the least of them unto the greatest of them,** saith the Lord. (King James Version)

There cannot possibly be a "least" and a "greatest" among men who all are "created equal."

One pundit who was consulted for some valid Christian reference to support the notion that "all men are created equal" pointed to the Christian teaching of a Trinity, citing the equality of the Father, the Son, and the Holy Ghost as ample Christian foundation for equality in all men. Then what scriptural foundation is there for the Trinity?

None.

Steven Ritchie, in a *Pillar of Truth* article, "The Origin of the Trinity," cites authoritative source after definitive source admitting of no Biblical reference to any such divine conglomerate:

The Illustrated Bible Dictionary records: "The word Trinity is not found in the Bible... . It did not find a place formally in the theology of the church till the 4th century."

The New Catholic Encyclopedia admits that the Trinity "is not ... directly and immediately the word of God."

The Encyclopedia of Religion and Ethics records: "At first the Christian Faith was not Trinitarian ... . It was not so in the apostolic and sub-apostolic ages, as reflected in the New Testament and other early Christian writings."

L. L. Paine, professor of Ecclesiastical History acknowledged: "The Old Testament is strictly monotheistic. God is a single personal being. The idea that a trinity is to be found there ... is utterly without foundation."

The Encyclopedia of Religion admits: "Theologians today are in agreement that the Hebrew Bible does not contain a doctrine of the Trinity."

The New Catholic Encyclopedia also admits: "The doctrine of the Holy Trinity is not taught in the Old Testament."

Jesuit Edmund Fortman wrote in his book, *The Triune God:* "There is no evidence that any sacred writer even suspected the existence of a Trinity within the Godhead ... . Even to see in the Old Testament suggestions or foreshadowings or "veiled signs" of the trinity of persons, is to go beyond the words and intent of the sacred writers."

The Encyclopedia of Religion says: "Theologians agree that the New Testament also does not contain an explicit doctrine of the Trinity."

The New Encyclopedia Britannica reports: "Neither the word Trinity nor the explicit doctrine appears in the New Testament."

The New International Dictionary of New Testament Theology confirms: "The New Testament does not contain the developed doctrine of the Trinity."

Trinitarians commonly whip out a Bible and flip to Matthew 28:19, thumping it with finality:

Go ye therefore, and teach all nations, baptizing them in the name of the Father, and of the Son, and of the Holy Ghost. (King James Version)

The validity of that passage's integrity to the original text of Matthew has been questioned and re-questioned often and volubly, and the website Biblical Unitarian presents a concise summary of the historical foundation for seriously questioning it:

Eusebius (c. 260—c. 340) was the Bishop of Caesarea and is known as "the Father of Church History." Although he wrote prolifically, his most celebrated work is his *Ecclesiastical History,* a history of the Church from the Apostolic period until his own time. Today it is still the principal work on the history of the Church at that time. Eusebius quotes many verses in his writings, and Matthew 28:19 is one of them. He never quotes it as it appears today in modern Bibles, but always finishes the verse with the words "in my name."

... If Matthew 28:19 is accurate as it stands in modern versions, then there is no explanation for the apparent disobedience of the apostles, since there is not a single occurrence of them baptizing anyone according to that formula. All the records in the New Testament show that people were baptized into the name of the Lord Jesus, just as the text Eusebius was quoting said to do.

The history of the evolution of the concept of a Christian Trinity had its roots in Egyptian and polytheistic beliefs, arguably taking *official* Christian form and shape only in the Nicene Creed, over three centuries after the birth of Jesus of Nazareth. (Use of apologetic language such as "arguably" in this manuscript is, regrettably, inescapable because some of our most vaunted academics and "experts" make entire careers out of fighting like the Kilkenny cats over conflicting theories. In fact, it's no longer even possible to get a degree without manufacturing some new "theory" about something, or rehashing somebody else's leftover theory so it looks like a new theory. We all have to deal with the mess that's left, and this topic of Trinitarism is no exception.)

The source of the term "Trinity" was Tertullian (c. 160-230), who coined the word *trinitas,* from which the English term "trinity" derives—but even he made particular note of differences amongst the three postulated polytheist/Christian divine partners of the so-called Trinity.

Tertullian built a careful, if convoluted, case for *his* theory:

The mystery of the divine economy should be safeguarded, which of the unity makes a trinity, placing the three in order not of quality but of sequence, different not in substance but in aspect, not in power but in manifestation.

(In trying to reconcile the irreconcilable, Tertullian may have simultaneously founded the field of Public Relations spin, but that's another story.)

The final authority on the "Trinity" issue, though, has to be the Judeo-Christian Creator himself, who seems to put an end to all question of his having any equal by asking his own pointed Zen-like questions, in Isaiah 40:25:

> To whom then will ye liken me, or shall I be equal? saith the Holy One. (King James Version)

There is only one possible answer: Nobody. This same Judeo-Christian Creator makes that unequivocally clear a little further on, in Isaiah 46:9 (bold emphasis added):

> Remember the former things of old: for I *am* God, and *there is* none else; **I am God, and *there is* none like me**. (King James Version)

The Trinity, then, must be ejected from debate, along with any foolish idea that the Abrahamic god Yahweh ever had an equal, or ever created men who were "equal."

Where, then, in all of Christendom is there any authority, any foundation, any crust of substantiation and validation for the outré declaration that "all men are created equal?"

As early as 1558, over 200 years before Jefferson penned his "created equal" assertion, a Scottish Christian theologian named John Knox wrote a "Letter Addressed to the Commonalty of Scotland" in which he made a tied-in-knots attempt to claim that all men, from kings to commoners, were somehow "equal," but he ended up confessing that any such "equality" only applied as an extortion to proselytize Christianity—effectively shutting out the rest of the world:

> And this is that equality which is betwixt the kings and subjects, the most rich or noble, and betwixt the poorest and men of lowest estate: to wit, that as the one is obliged to believe in heart, and with mouth to confess, the Lord Jesus to be the only Saviour of the world, so also is the other.

Knox no doubt evolved his convoluted theory from scripture such as Galatians 3:26–28, bold emphasis added:

> 26 For ye are all the children of God **by faith in Christ Jesus.**
> 27 For as many of you **as have been baptized into Christ have put on Christ.**
> 28 There is neither Jew nor Greek, there is neither bond nor free, there is neither male nor female: for **ye are all one in Christ Jesus.**

In short: those who have been baptized into Christ are equal in that specific sense—but those who have not been so anointed are not. Knox's knock-off boils down to a self-authorizing authoritarian decree that conveniently ignores all scriptural evidence to the contrary—while simultaneously describing classifications of very *unequal* human beings in order to make the case for there existing some kind of "equality." (If it seems that you're riding a philosophical merry-go-round in trying to follow Knox, you're right. Circularity is always a mind trap.)

Even attempts at finding a latter-day reasoned discussion of ways in which pieces and snippets of Hebrew or Christian scripture might somehow be cobbled together and synthesized into a cogent thesis that the Judeo-Christian god actually intended for all of humankind to be "created equal" turned up only this other circular mind trap from *Prodigal Nation—Part 1,* by Reverend Peter Marshall:

> The idea that all men are created equal comes ... from Genesis 1:27 ("And God created man in His own image"). How do we know that all men are created equal? Because all men bear the image of God, and therefore all men are of equal value to God.

If Reverend Marshall would take some time to brush up on his scripture beyond the first chapter, he would discover that the Judeo-Christian god himself made reference to a certain man having no equal among other men (1 Kings 3:12-13), and expressly proclaimed that there were differences among men, from "the least of them to the greatest of them" (Jeremiah 31:34).

Any attempt to then reconcile or combine the two biblical mandates that (a) the Judeo-Christian God himself has *no equal* (Isaiah 40:25–46:9), and, (b) He created man in *His own image* (Genesis 1:27), creates a spinning whirly-gig for the mind, a veritable cyclotron of illogic, in which you can chase your own tail until Gabriel blows his horn trying to prove that "all men are created equal" by this entirely *un*equaled Judeo-Christian god. (You might want to read this paragraph several times if you feel dizzy.)

It is patently impossible to pin this weird "created equal" dogma on Abraham's god Yahweh/Jehovah. He cannot possibly be the culprit called "Nature's God." Not guilty. Case dismissed.

Then what's left?

Well—

Nothing.

There's nothing at all left but a bold, assertive, and contextually truncated proclamation by a relatively small collection of fallible men whose abbreviated, if well-intended, shout charted a course for civilization to follow for centuries: "WE hold these truths to be self-evident: that all men are created equal."

Is that *it?*

Is that wreckage of irrationality the entire foundation for this fixed idea?

Is that single arbitrary, absolutist, authoritarian proclamation the *total argument?*

Is *that one sentence* really the *entire scope* of "reason and rationale" that has led mankind:

to launch a thousand steam-rolling, person-leveling legislative bills;

to sculpt or pound other cultures or civilizations into our own self-proclaimed god-imprinted cookie-cutter image;

to impress on children that the best they can become is the worst that they witness;

to force incompatible cultures, religions, and nations into quietly resentful, falsely jolly intercourse;

to nudge men toward womanhood and women toward manhood;

to fill vital agencies and businesses with rude, ignorant, arrogant (but "equal") wage drudges;

to gag employers with orders not to ask any qualifying question that might actually distinguish one human being from another;

to reduce literacy standards down to vulgar street jargon;

to lavish costly "entitlements" on the least able and least productive in the society;

to drive taxes ever higher for subsidizing sloth;

to promote into "leadership" cheaters and embezzlers;

to let accident-prone louts drive cars, then inflate the police rolls to enforce auto insurance;

to glut the newsstands and media with the gee-whiz musings of pompous simpletons;

to reduce every living being to a faceless "human resource," a commodity like so much cordwood;

to celebrate sameness;

to graduate mediocrity;

to incubate conformity;

to cultivate passivity;

to denigrate refinement;

to elevate degradation?

Is this vapid "created equal" proclamation the *sole justification* for such societal madness?

Can it be?

Apparently so.

Just five simple words, "all men are created equal," and—Poof!— spontaneous equality.

That this batty statement was endorsed by a group of men as being a "truth" held to be "self-evident" is the *entire foundation* not only for its blind, unquestioning acceptance, but for its wholesale, bloody, catastrophic gallop across the face of history.

It is the greatest lie.

And though that is bad enough, it is not the worst philosophical felony. No, the real felony is far more foul.

Clues to the felony are found through the work of a learned and erudite contemporary of Jefferson, the sometimes saturnine but meticulously authoritative wordsmith and word-keeper, Samuel Johnson. His landmark first dictionary of the English language had been published in two volumes 20 years before the *Declaration of Independence* was unleashed upon the world.

In 1776, Johnson's work was the definitive reference on the

definitions of English words. Here is what his dictionary provided for all the relevant forms of "create":

To CREA'TE. *v. a. [creo, Lat.]* To form out of nothing; to cause to exist. *Genesis.* To produce; to cause. *Shakespeare.* To beget. To invest with any new character. *Shakespeare.* To give any new qualities. *Davies.*

CREA'TED. *a.* Begotten. *Shakespeare.* Composed; made up. *Ibid.*

CREA'TION. *n. s.* The act of creating. Bp. *Taylor.* The act of investing with new qualities or character; as, the creation of peers. The universe. *Denham.* Anything produced, or caused. *Shakespeare*

CREA'TIVE. *a.* Having the power to create. *Thomson.* Exerting the act of creation. *South.*

CREA'TOR. *n. s. [Lat.]* The being that bestows existence. *Milton.*

In writing those five words into the *Declaration of Independence*, "all men are created equal," Thomas Jefferson created—*formed out of nothing, caused to exist, invested with new qualities and character*—a fantastical and grotesque myth, an entirely fictitious new breed of men that engulfed all mankind: men who all are "created equal."

By *whom*?

Never, before the *Declaration of Independence*, in the entire long history of religion around the world, had anyone even heard of this "Creator" called "Nature's God."

Thomas Jefferson, despite speculation by some, never claimed that he was a deist, so "Nature's God" is not a made-up name for a deist deity. Jefferson referred to himself as a Unitarian. Unitarianism is a Christian religious movement whose central creed—and even its very name—rejects the idea of a holy Trinity, asserting that the Judeo-Christian god is a *single* deity. That's Yahweh, and Yahweh has been ruled herein as "not guilty" of creating all men "equal." Neither the Judeo-Christian god, nor any other god of record, nor even a cosmic explosion, ever breathed into existence an army of "created equal" clones, as claimed in the *Declaration of Independence*. So *who* was it?

It was Jefferson himself.

And however disturbing that thought might be, that yet is not the *real* philosophical felony.

Jefferson quietly evaded responsibility for his own creation of "created equal" men. Although he used a fabricated name, "Nature's God," he *tacitly* let the Judeo-Christian god take the blame, and *the Judeo-Christian god didn't do it.*

And that still is not the real felony. But it's very close. Because with Jefferson taking no personal responsibility for having created a new breed of cloned men, and with the Judeo-Christian god Yahweh having been proven conclusively to be "not guilty," that leaves a missing Creator. It leaves a vacuum where a Creator has to be.

The real felony, then, is that Jefferson created a non-existent "Creator" who allegedly created all men equal, and Jefferson presented this haint, this apparition, this no-see-um, as being "Nature's God."

Jefferson created the Creator.

4. The Man Behind the Curtain
In Whose Image?

Thomas Jefferson dreamed up the generic name "Nature's God," but was Jefferson really the mastermind behind the philosophical felony of manufacturing a phony "Creator" who supposedly created all men "equal"? Or was Jefferson merely a credulous accomplice who had, himself, been lulled into loving a lie?

Who *actually* created the Creator that is costumed in the *Declaration of Independence* as "Nature's God," looming over mankind like the giant projected apparition in the *Wizard of Oz?* The worldwide fame of the *Declaration of Independence* catapulted the "created equal" dogma into global consciousness and blind-faith acceptance, but that is by no means its genesis—for want of a better term. So *where* did it start? *Who* is the original author? What *man* among men created the alleged "Creator" that supposedly—if impossibly—created all men as "equal"?

Who is the man behind the curtain?

It's a 17th-century asthmatically fey, affected, effeminate, and feeble "philosopher" named John Locke.

Almost a century before Thomas Jefferson sat down to write the *Declaration of Independence*, John Locke had conjured up his fabulous fantasy of a "God" or "Maker" who, according to Locke, had created all men as "equal." It could be said that Locke wrote the first science fiction: a world populated by beings who are "equal and independent." He might as well have said we all are robots from the same assembly line—and he was two centuries ahead of H. G. Wells, Jules Verne, or Hugo Gernsback.

The mysterious "Creator" that Thomas Jefferson later evoked—the "Creator" called "Nature's God" in the *Declaration of Independence*—was nothing more than the very same mystical "Maker" that John Locke had fabricated decades earlier in his febrile fantasies. All evidence points straight to John Locke as the *source* of the outré idea that "all men are created equal," Locke's exact words being: "mankind ... being all equal and independent." In Jefferson's first draft of the *Declaration of Independence* he wrote, "all men are created equal & independant" [sic], unquestionably echoing Locke—without attribution—and Jefferson's appeal to "the Laws of Nature & of Nature's God" was straight out of the works of Locke.

John Locke's *Second Treatise of Government* was published nearly 90 years before the *Declaration of Independence*—in late 1689 (with a title-page date of 1690). It said (bold emphasis added):

> The **law of nature** stands as an eternal rule to all men, legislators as well as others. The rules that they make for other men's actions, must, as well as their own and other men's actions, be conformable to the **laws of nature, i.e. to the will of God** ... .
>
> The **state of nature has a law of nature to govern it,** which obliges every one: and **reason, which is that law,** teaches **all mankind** ... that **being all equal and independent,** no one ought to harm another in his **life,** health, **liberty, or possessions**: for **men being all the workmanship of one omnipotent, and infinitely wise Maker** ... .

There are so many deadly traps of illogic in that dense tar pit of tortured syntax that much of the rest of this book is devoted to plotting a safe and sane path through them, but for the moment, compare Jefferson's original draft of the *Declaration of Independence* (capitalization and spelling as in original, bold emphasis added):

> When in the course of human events it becomes necessary for a people ... to assume among the powers of the earth the **equal & independant** [sic] station to which **the laws of nature & of nature's god** entitle them, a decent respect to the opinions of mankind requires that they should declare the causes which impel them to the change.
>
> We hold these truths to be sacred & undeniable; that **all men are created equal & independant** [sic], that from that **equal creation** they derive **rights** inherent & inalienable, among which are the preservation of

life, & **liberty,** & the pursuit of happiness.

These compared passages demonstrate conclusively that:

1) In the original draft of the *Declaration of Independence,* Jefferson's profoundly obtuse use of the phrase "all men are created equal & independant" [sic] unquestionably arose from Jefferson's contact with the bloated prose and murmuring mind of John Locke.

2) In the final draft of the *Declaration of Independence,* the simpleminded sentiment that "all men are created equal" is nothing more than a restatement of one of John Locke's many preposterous proclamations. It's science fiction, politicized.

3) Jefferson made up a name, "Nature's God"—the way you might name a sock puppet—and assigned that name to some nonexistent and nebulous "Creator" that had never existed before in any known religion. In doing so, Jefferson was merely giving a contrived name to the *same nonexistent and nebulous "Maker"* that John Locke had manufactured from fantasy as the alleged "Creator" of something extremely vague that Locke called "nature's laws"—which purported "laws" Locke *never bothered to list or define.* [Much more about Locke's failure at defining "law of nature" in later chapters. —Ed.]

Fans, students, and "experts" of Locke very likely are bristling in disagreement at this point, ready to launch a fusillade of furious fits and fussing to insist that Locke was invoking the Judeo-Christian god, Yahweh, as the "Creator" of all-equal men. Well, tamp down your temper temporarily, because we've already proved conclusively that Yahweh—according to the only record that exists, purportedly His own Word—absolutely did not create all men "equal," and in a moment we're going to discover, just as conclusively, that Locke was not a Christian at all.

Locke's writings had gained considerable currency in the Jeffersonian era, particularly among some of the "enlighteners" of the intellectual movement that is colloquially (and generously) called "The Enlightenment." There is not the slightest question that John Locke was Jefferson's source and muse: Jefferson is on record specifically naming John Locke as one of "the three greatest men that have ever lived, without any exception," the other two, in his estimation, being Francis Bacon and Isaac Newton.

A few "authorities," including John F. Kennedy and the United States Congress (following Kennedy), have falsely claimed that Jefferson took the "created equal" doctrine from a lesser-light named Phillip Mazzei:

> The great doctrine "All men are created equal" and [sic] incorporated into the *Declaration of Independence* by Thomas Jefferson, was paraphrased from the writing of Philip Mazzei, an Italian-born patriot and pamphleteer, who was a close friend of Jefferson. **—John F. Kennedy,** *A Nation of Immigrants*

The claim is insupportable and false, given that Mazzei wasn't even born until 1730—26 years after Locke's death, and 41 years after Locke's "equal and independent" dogma had been published. Just because Mazzei embraced and parroted Locke doesn't make Mazzei Jefferson's source; the source for both Mazzei and Jefferson unquestionably was Locke.

Several of the ever-dueling "experts" have accused Jefferson of downright plagiarism, but there is no evidence to make any damning case that Jefferson—or Mazzei, for that matter—knowingly, willfully "plagiarized" Locke, and Jefferson himself addressed this issue directly during the last few years of his life:

> Whether I had gathered my ideas from reading or reflection I do not know. I know only that I turned to neither book nor pamphlet while writing it. I did not consider it as any part of my charge to invent new ideas altogether, and to offer no sentiment which had ever been expressed before.
> **Thomas Jefferson**—30 August 1823, letter to James Madison

> This was the object of the *Declaration of Independence*. Not to find out new principles, or new arguments, never before thought of, not merely to say

things which have never been said before; but to place before mankind the common sense of the subject, in terms so plain and firm as to command their assent, and to justify ourselves in the independent stand we are compelled to take. Neither aiming at originality of principle or sentiment, nor yet copied from any particular or previous writing, it was intended to be an expression of the American mind, and to give that expression the proper tone and spirit called for by the occasion. All its authority rests then on the harmonizing sentiments of the day, whether expressed in conversation, letters, printed essays, or in the elementary books of public right, as Aristotle, Cicero, Locke, Sidney, etc.

Thomas Jefferson—8 May 1825, letter to Henry Lee

If there is a dose of plagiarism poisoning this stew, it isn't Jefferson's; it came from Locke's own twisted garden of wordy weeds—about which more will be said later. The mistake of Jefferson and his contemporaries was to pick judiciously from Locke's works what they thought to be golden fruit from the tree of shared human knowledge; what they bit into was pure poison.

Most historians agree, with little argument (there's a surprise), that it was Thomas Jefferson who penned those pregnant five words, "all men are created equal," at the home of Jacob Graff. There is uncertainty about whether Jefferson was a willing party to the later addition of the word "Creator." There was no mention of "Creator" in his first draft.

Still, Jefferson himself must be held accountable for using the word "created," and for pinning such alleged creation on some made-up, fictional entity that he called "Nature's God." Jefferson was following Locke's lead—if only into a murky, impenetrable, Stygian darkness—because Locke maddeningly evaded any direct, unequivocal answer to the question of who this "God" was who supposedly created all men "equal."

Now that we've gotten the actual source of this "created equal" dogma in our sights, now that we know who created the false "Creator" who supposedly created all men "equal," it's necessary to look into Locke a little and the system of his beliefs. As might be imagined already, it becomes an adventure into a world as surreal as a Salvador Dali landscape.

Locke's Religion—Or Irreligion—That Created Everyone as "Equal"

Locke *ostensibly* was Christian in faith and practice, but it could not have been more than lip-service, a "faith" of convenience, a "faith" of social and political practicality in 17th-century England, where the Established Church of England was the official religion and the only true "orthodoxy." As of December 1661, for example, no one could even hold an official city or corporate position in England without having taken sacraments of the Church of England and a variety of vows.

But Locke was no Christian. He pretended to be, and did a poor job even at that. In fact, Locke was a closet omnitheist, or omnist, or pantheist, or deist—or some vacillating combination of all the foregoing—well before some of those words even came into the language. This has been lying in plain sight since his first published work, haughtily titled "A Letter Concerning Toleration," in which he said:

> Try when you please with a bramin [sic: Brahmin, Hindu], a mahometan [Muslim], a papist [Catholic], lutheran, quaker, anabaptist, presbyterian, &c. you will find ... that you are no more a judge for any of them than they are for you. Men in all religions have equally strong persuasions, and every one must judge for himself; nor can any one judge for another.

Although that is "officially" considered his first published work (by the "experts"), in fact an earlier work of his, unattributed at the time, stands as stunning proof of his complete indifference to Christianity and the Judeo-Christian God. It is the "Fundamental Constitutions of Carolina." In it he wrote (bold emphasis added):

> No man shall be permitted to be a freeman of Carolina, or to have any estate or habitation within it, that doth not acknowledge **a God**, and **that God** is publicly to be worshipped. ... **Any seven or more persons, agreeing in any religion, shall constitute a church** or profession [of religious belief] to which they shall give some name to distinguish it from others.

Pick a god, any god. In short, Locke's "religion" could have been summed up succinctly as "All of men's gods are created equal by all men"—which provides the complete explanation for why he ducked and hid from the question of what "Maker" would have, or could have, created all men "equal." It also rides the same perpetual merry-go-round as his barking-mad decree that all men are "equal and independent"—which would mean, of course, that all men create all their gods as equal and independent. And then all of those equal-and-independent gods create all men as equal and independent, so that those equally created men can then create gods for themselves that all are equal and independent, and then those gods therefore create all men as equal and independent. And it goes round and round and round eternally, forever, *ad infinitum, ad nauseum.* Really, Locke had out-paganed all the pagans, or polytheists, who ever existed—while pretending to monotheism—because he allowed for the infinite creation of an infinite number of gods by any group of seven persons or more.

It isn't that Locke's embracive, if supercilious, "tolerance" for every god ever conjured up is worthy of disdain, but his hypocrisy in simultaneously masquerading as "a true Christian" is beyond disdain.

Locke was far too evasive and hypocritical ever to come right out and declare his waffling antipathy toward Christianity, going so far as to write a windy, wordy, mincing apologia called "The Reasonableness of Christianity"—none of which is remotely reasonable, all of which is "Christian" only in the number of verses Locke cherry-picked from the Bible to make dubious declarations. It was in the introduction that he christened himself "a true Christian." The very title of the work bespeaks an unspeakable arrogance, Locke perching himself on the highest moral ground to hand down his "approval" (well, more or less) of over 1,600 years of Christian thought and practice. Much of it is an aloof, clucking disappointment at Yahweh's miserable creation-failure named Adam, and the sorry lot (pun unavoidable) Adam left to the rest of us as a result of his miserable failings by taking a bite from the Tree of Life. Lest anyone who has had the good grace to escape direct contact with the works of Locke thinks I'm misrepresenting the facts, here are some excerpts, stripped of Locke's incoherent padding and filler:

> The doctrine of redemption, and consequently of the gospel, is founded upon the supposition of Adam's fall. ... What Adam fell from (is visible) was the state of perfect obedience ... and by this fall he lost paradise, wherein was tranquillity [sic] and the tree of life; i.e. he lost bliss and immortality. ... He did eat: but, in the day he did eat, he did not actually die; but was turned out of paradise from the tree of life, and shut out for ever from it, lest he should take thereof, and live for ever. This shows, that the state of paradise was a state of immortality, of life without end; which he lost that very day that he eat ... . death came on all men by Adam's sin ... .
>
> Paradise was a place of bliss, as well as immortality; without drudgery, and without sorrow. But, when man was turned out, he was exposed to the toil, anxiety, and frailties of this mortal life ...
>
> As Adam was turned out of paradise, so all his posterity were born out of it, out of the reach of the tree of life; all, like their father Adam, in a state of mortality, void of the tranquility and bliss of paradise. ...
>
> Adam being thus turned out of paradise, and all his posterity born out of it, the consequence of it was, that all men should die, and remain under death for ever, and so be utterly lost.

According to Locke, if Adam hadn't taken that fateful bite *everyone born since* would still be alive today, but somehow in a state of "bliss," immortal, "without drudgery, and without sorrow." He doesn't mention that it would be standing-room-only on every square inch of this "paradise." This, according to Locke, is "reasonableness."

Locke also never reaches the obvious conclusion that if we're all "created equal," and Adam was a miserable failure, then he, Locke, is as miserable a failure as Adam. He goes through a torturous and tedious attempt to explain that away by categorizing Adam as a one-and-only exception. Here's a brief, if painful, glimpse at Locke's "reasonableness":

> Adam being the Son of God, and so St. Luke calls him, chap. iii. 38, had this part also of the likeness and image of his father, viz. that he was immortal. But Adam, transgressing the command given him by his heavenly Father, incurred the penalty; forfeited that state of immortality, and became mortal. After this, Adam begot children: but they were "in his own likeness, after his own image;" mortal, like their father.

Great. So it's all Adam's fault, and "his heavenly Father" *just happened* to give Adam *the one and only "command"* that Adam somehow had been too unblissful to obey—while in his state of eternal bliss. And that *one and only "command"* just happened to condemn all the rest of us to sin and death, unless and until we were rescued from it by "the second Adam," Jesus of Nazareth. "Reasonableness," according to John Locke.

The worst part of Locke's nails-on-a-blackboard screeching screed on Christianity is that it conveniently ignores the fact that Christianity, like every religion ever in existence, is a function of *faith*—not "reasonableness." It could very soundly be said that all religious faith—no matter what the religion—exists to fill in the gaps where reason fails. That is no condemnation of faith; on the contrary, that is affirmation of the vital necessity of faith, for without faith, the gaps where reason fails become the most abhorrent thing possible: a vacuum. That's why even the most materialistic materialist, even the most atheistic atheist, has fervent faith in no-see-ums such as synergy and gravity, neither of which he can explain.

But to John Locke, faith—*any* faith—was simply a mode of madness. I can almost hear the hair being self-ripped from the heads of fanboys of John Locke right now, so let no one take what I just said by my word. Here it is, verbatim, from the words of John Locke himself, in his private notes, this one dated 19 February 1682:

> A strong and firm persuasion of any proposition relating to religion, for which a man hath either no or not sufficient proofs from reason, but receives them as truths wrought in the mind extraordinarily by influence coming immediately from God himself, seems to me to be enthusiasm, which can be no evidence or ground of assurance at all, nor can by any means be taken for knowledge.
>
> If such groundless thoughts as these, concerning ordinary matters, and not religion, possess the mind strongly, we call it raving, and every one thinks it a degree of madness; but in religion, men, accustomed to the thoughts of revelation, make a greater allowance to it, though indeed it be a more dangerous madness; but men are apt to think in religion they may, and ought, to quit their reason.
>
> I find that the Christians, Mahometans [Muslims], and Brahmins [Hindus], all pretend to this immediate inspiration; but it is certain that contradictions and falsehoods cannot come from God; nor can any one that is of the true religion, be assured of any thing by a way whereof those of a false religion may be, and are equally confirmed in theirs. For the Turkish dervishes [Muslims] pretend to revelations, ecstasies, visions, raptures, to be transported with illumination of God ... . The Jaugis, amongst the Hindoos, talk of being illuminated and entirely united to God ... as well as the most spiritualized Christians.

There it is as bald as an onion: anything at all, by anyone—no matter what professed religion—that smacks of contact with God or with things spiritual, or even of belief in or awareness of God or things spiritual, is "raving," "a degree of madness," "a more dangerous madness" than any other. In short, faith is madness. And this begins to give us a sort of shivering glimmer of realization about what John Locke actually was. Hint: It wasn't Christian.

What Christian—who is actually a "true Christian"—needs John Locke to tell them how "reasonable" Christianity is? "The Reasonableness of Christianity" was so opaquely incomprehensible and self-contradictory that a contemporary critic called him out on it, and Locke then felt compelled to write not one, but two "vindications" of "The Reasonableness of Christianity"—neither of them being either vindications or reasonable or Christian. In the second "vindication," Locke attempted a sarcastic swipe at his critic, but in the very act inadvertently admitted how laughingly quasi-Christian his closet-heretic meanderings were:

> I [Locke] must be what he [the critic] thinks fit; when he pleases, a papist [Catholic]; and when he pleases, a socinian [a non-Trinitarian Christian splinter group]; and when he pleases, a mahometan [Muslim]: and probably, when he has considered a little better, an atheist.

As a matter of sober fact, the truth outs: Locke *was* an atheist. Even his condescending "tolerance" for all non-Christian "gods" was itself a form of lip-service, because beneath all the preening piety-of-convenience, Locke was a materialist, and it is patently impossible to be a materialist and also believe that man has a soul or spiritual existence. This is the electrified fence dividing materialism and spirituality (note: I did *not* say "spiritualism," about which more later), and it is not possible to straddle that fence. A 1913 definition by Constantin Gutberlet in Volume 10 of *The Catholic Encyclopedia* has it right:

> Materialism is a philosophical system which regards matter as the only reality in the world, which undertakes to explain every event in the universe as resulting from the conditions and activity of matter, and which thus denies the existence of God and the soul.

Many "experts" have come along since that time and tried to slice, dice, divide, subdivide, and sub-subdivide that simple and accurate definition, positing a host of different "brands" of materialism, trying to soft-pedal its anti-God, anti-soul component, but this issue is truly "one side or the other." Either the spiritual aspect of man's existence is part of the equation of life, or it isn't. Period. The perspicacious Will Durant, in his extraordinary work, *The Story of Philosophy*, demonstrated with impeccable logic how and why Locke was a materialist:

> [Locke] announced, quietly, that all our knowledge comes from experience and through our senses—that "there is nothing in the mind except what was first in the senses." The mind [according to Locke] is at birth a clean sheet, a *tabula rasa;* and sense-experience writes upon it in a thousand ways, until sensation begets memory and memory begets ideas. All of which seemed to lead to the startling conclusion that since only material things can effect our sense, we know nothing but matter, and must accept a materialistic philosophy.

Sir Isaac Newton—one of the two other men besides Locke who Thomas Jefferson considered to be "the three greatest men that have ever lived"—recognized that Locke was a materialist and an atheist, and actually said so, though it's been buried and wished away by the disciples of Locke. One of Newton's biographers, Frank E. Manuel, wastes far too much of his book, *A Portrait of Isaac Newton*, on pitifully amateurish attempts at long-distance time-travel Freudian analysis of Newton, but does document the fact that Newton accused Locke of being "a Hobbist, which meant a materialist and an atheist." Manuel claims that Newton said it in the fit of a mental breakdown, but even though Newton apologized after the fact, it likely was among his most lucid and astute observations. (It should be noted that the quarrel between Locke and Newton took place in private correspondence, made public only many years after their deaths, and there is no reason to believe that Thomas Jefferson ever learned of it.)

Locke was the Grand High Wizard of materialism. Locke was an atheist in Christian disguise. Locke's materialism and its disciples have turned the world and mankind to tar. And it's tar from there on down. Now, in light of this knowledge, let's briefly revisit that

Lockean tar pit quoted at the beginning of this chapter, the one that Jefferson and friends got their feet stuck in, and peer through his pompous piety to what lies beneath:

> The **law of nature** stands as an eternal rule to all men, legislators as well as others. The rules that they make for other men's actions, must, as well as their own and other men's actions, be conformable to the **laws of nature, i.e. to the will of God** ... .
>
> The **state of nature has a law of nature to govern it,** which obliges every one: and **reason, which is that law,** teaches **all mankind** ... that **being all equal and independent,** no one ought to harm another in his **life,** health, **liberty, or possessions**: for **men being all the workmanship of one omnipotent, and infinitely wise Maker** ... .

There, revealed, is an awe-inspiring example of the man's worminess with words. Even the most devious lawyer would have to be impressed.

Note that he does not directly say the "law of God," nor does he anywhere in the piece *unequivocally* declare that the Judeo-Christian god Yahweh was the "God" with the "will," or was the "omnipotent, and infinitely wise Maker" behind creating this alleged "law of nature." His ambiguity has you already knee-deep in the tar—and you're there whether you are Christian or Wiccan or with the Cult of Kek. Then Locke springs the ultimate trap: he claims that man's ability to *reason—the ability to think and draw conclusions—*is the *sum and totality* of this alleged "law of nature"—which he claims is "the will of God." Some God.

But wait: in his notes quoted earlier, he declared that "truths wrought in the mind extraordinarily by influence coming immediately from God himself" were ravings, and dangerous madness. So how, then, could Locke possibly know that "reason" was the "will of God" without it being a "truth wrought" in his own mind "by influence coming immediately from God himself"? But that would mean that Locke was—well, mad.

And now you're not only hip-deep in the tar, you're riding the Lockean Merry-Go-Round to Nowhere in the tar. And it's sinking. Fast. Just one reason it's such a deadly trap is that it forces every person reading such madness to guess or conclude *subjectively—using his own "reason"*—what the "law of nature" or "law of God" is, and what "God" ordained it.

But wait: If we go back to Locke's "Reasonableness of Christianity," that would have to mean, inescapably, that Adam had been given this ability to *reason* by his "infinitely wise Maker." And when Adam used his *reason*, he *reasoned* that the best thing he could do was take a bite from the forbidden fruit. And that condemned us all.

But wait: According to Locke, that "reason" that Adam used is the "law of nature," which also is "the will of God." Which can only mean, inescapably, that God intentionally rigged Adam's ability to reason so he would make the most deadly decision possible. And that, according to Locke, is an "eternal rule" to guide "all men."

And as you bubble down into the black, sticky, no-escape mire of Lockean lunacy, going round and round and round, your last *thought* is, "Oh: all men are created equal." And you drown in the tar of materialism. John Locke was *not* a Christian. He pretended to be, and he used the language of "God" and the Bible—writing primarily for Christians of every description in his era—the way a carnival barker uses "We have a winna'!"

BRIEF ASIDE TO READER: Do you feel that "lunacy" in the paragraph above is irresponsible and incendiary language, not appropriate to any scholarly and balanced and unbiased analysis of Locke and his works? Do you feel that already I'm being far too harsh, or unfairly critical or judgmental of John Locke? Here's my problem, dear reader: I have the benefit—or perhaps the curse—of already knowing what else is going to be revealed about Locke in the rest of this book, and honestly, it's all I can do to refrain from using language my mother could never have approved of. In fact, I am exercising, right this moment, extreme restraint to keep this account within some boundaries of civility. But if you will bear with me, I would be willing to wager that by the time you finish this book, you, too, will be tempted toward language about Locke that you might not want to say in front of your own mother. With that, we will forge ahead—

so forgive me if my restraint at times slips to something less than saintly. I forgive you in advance if yours does, too.

A revelatory indication of Locke's own deep-seated aversion to a life of Christian devotion is the incident of his willful deceit and machinations in weaseling out of obligations of service in religious orders, chronicled by H. R. Fox Bourne in his two-volume biography, *The Life of John Locke,* published in 1876. There's no need for a dry, dusty deliberation or rehash of the life of Locke and its historical context—there are too many bleached bones of predecessors that would have to be walked on to take that route. But there are some insights into Locke's character that are well worth taking a look at.

The incident at issue took place in November 1666, after Locke had been studying for a number of years at Christ Church, Oxford, England. Locke had failed to take the necessary steps to achieve a degree in medicine, a field he had dabbled in, and as a result of his negligence—or sloth—he was faced with having no choice, based on prevailing rules and regulations, but to go into the clergy. For an account of Locke's underhandedness, it's impossible to improve on Mr. Bourne's biography, so let him tell it:

> On the 3rd of November, 1666, a year after the time when, in the ordinary course, he [Locke] might have obtained the degree of doctor in physic, he procured from the Earl of Clarendon, then chancellor of the university, a document of great significance. Addressing Dr. Fell, the vice-chancellor, and the several heads of houses, Clarendon thus wrote:
>
> > "Mr. Vice-Chancellor and Gentlemen,
> > "I am very well assured that Mr. John Locke, a master of arts and student of Christ Church, has employed his time in the study of physic to so good purpose that he is in all respects qualified for the degree of doctor in that faculty, for which he has also full time; but, having not taken the degree of bachelor in physic, he has desired that he may be dispensed with to accumulate that degree, which appears to me a very modest and reasonable request, he professing himself ready to perform the exercise for both degrees. I therefore very willingly give my consent that a dispensation to that purpose be propounded for him.
> > "Mr. Vice-Chancellor and Gentlemen,
> > "Your very affectionate servant,
> > "Clarendon."

That recommendation, almost equivalent to a command, was, strange to say, not attended to. Honorary degrees of all sorts were in these years given away in abundance at Oxford, and in this case the highest authority in the university vouched that the degree need only be an honorary one because certain formalities had been neglected: yet the chancellor's instruction was not heeded. It is evident that already adverse influences against Locke were at work. The high church party was dominant at Oxford; and Locke was not a high churchman. ...

Oh, this is by no means the end of Locke's backroom bamboozling that November, but it is instructive here to pause in this narrative for a word about the Earl of Clarendon, whose missive and mission somehow failed. He was Edward Hyde, the 1st Earl of Clarendon, and at the time of this event, quite in addition to his being Chancellor of Oxford, he was the Chief Minister of England under King Charles II, an office of mercurial scope and power, but powerful and close to the king, nonetheless. It is senseless to think that someone of John Locke's low-rung status and standing could have bumped into Clarendon in a hallway and asked for a pass. Somebody—*somebody*—was pulling heavy strings for Locke. But who? Who could have had such influence? And why would they use it for Locke? Well, stay tuned. Now back to Bourne's account ...

Eleven days later, doubtless on finding that Clarendon's request would be ignored by the university authorities, he [Locke] obtained another document, and one that no university opposition could overrule. This did not directly assist him in the medical career that he had marked out for himself; but it enabled him to retain the Christ Church studentship, which he had lately been holding in an irregular way, and from which, now that he had finally abandoned all thought of becoming a clergyman, it is probable that some effort was being made to oust him. The document, marked in the margin, "Dispensation for Mr. Locke," and addressed "To our trusty, etc., the dean and chapter of Christ Church, in our university of Oxford," was as follows:

"Trusty, etc.,

"Whereas we are informed that John Locke, master of arts and student of Christ Church, in our university of Oxford, is of such standing as by the custom of that college he is obliged to enter into holy orders or otherwise to leave his student's place there, at his humble request that he may still have further time to prosecute his studies without that obligation, we are graciously pleased to grant him our royal dispensation, and do accordingly hereby require you to suffer him, the said John Locke, to hold and enjoy his said student's place in Christ Church, together with all the rights, profits, and emoluments thereunto belonging, without taking holy orders upon him according to the custom of the college or any rule of the students in that case, with which we are graciously pleased to dispense in that behalf. And for so doing this shall be your warrant. Given at our court at Whitehall, the 14th day of November, 1666, in the eighteenth year of our reign.

"By his majesty's command,

"William Morrice"

[NOTE: Bourne has the name as "Morrice." So do many records at British History Online—but that source also has the name as "Morice." The name in Samuel Pepys's diaries, in genealogies, and in many other accounts is "Morice." This book will use "Morice" going forward.—Ed.]

That dispensation, signed by [King] Charles the Second's secretary of state, was of great advantage to Locke during the years in which it was allowed to have force. It was of immediate benefit in enabling him, instead of going out into the world in search of other occupation, to remain at the university, and to pursue his studies in medical and kindred subjects.

Even a dull reader might well be wondering, right about now, how in the world this slip-shodding "student" managed to get such a stupefyingly regal command on his behalf issued by such a highly placed official in the court of the reigning king of all England, Scotland, and Ireland—and not just from one royal official, but from *two,* all within less than two weeks. It's a thudding good question, and it's almost equally stupefying that the biographer Bourne never bothered to offer an explanation. Neither have any of Locke's many biographers or fawning fans. It's about time somebody did, and the most obvious answer is one that Locke's disciples are understandably coy about mentioning.

It is certain, though, that both the original letter from Clarendon, and the magisterial "dispensation" from William Morice, were quietly arranged by a man who at the time was, himself, very powerful and influential in English politics: Anthony Ashley Cooper—Lord Ashley, who later became 1st Earl of Shaftesbury, and thereby Lord Shaftesbury. (The "Lord Ashley" and "Lord Shaftesbury" monikers are used interchangeably in much of the literature, depending on when it was written. Some of such literature is quoted here, which can create its own confusion, so realize they are the same man, and further references to Lord Ashley/Lord Shaftesbury in this text will be indifferent to when he became a Baron, as Lord Ashley, versus when he became an Earl, as Lord Shaftesbury.)

On 20 April 1661—five years before this incident with Locke and the letters—King Charles II had elevated Anthony Ashley Cooper to Lord Ashley, or Baron Ashley, of Wimborne St. Giles, permitting him to serve in the House of Lords. Less than a month later, on 11 May 1661, Ashley had been appointed to the post of Chancellor of the Exchequer of England. The position is today counted among the "Four Great Offices of State" in England's history, and it put Ashley in close association with Clarendon and William Morice. Such was the position and status of Ashley in November 1666, when these letters were written for Locke. But the question remains: Why would someone in the position of Lord Ashley be doing such high-level favors for Locke?

Ashley had traveled to Oxford just a few months *earlier* than this incident with the letters, arriving there in July 1666, seeking treatment in the form of medicinal waters that were available there. While in Oxford he met Locke. The meeting came about because Locke was acting as nothing more than an errand boy to bring some of the mystical waters to Ashley; it was a favor for a mutual friend who was not able to make the delivery as he had expected to do. Those must have been some mystical waters, indeed—or Love Potion No. 9—to listen to accounts of how Locke locked onto Ashley, and Ashley locked onto Locke, in their very first encounter, near the end of July 1666. A blushing account of the encounter and the resulting relationship was given into record by a contemporary of the two men named Damaris Cudworth, Lady Masham, who wrote (bold emphasis added):

> Those who knew my Lord Shaftesbury did never represent Mr. Locke to themselves as a man more extraordinary than when they recalled to their remembrance the singular esteem my Lord Shaftesbury had of him. That two such persons should find an uncommon delight in the company of each other is not to be wondered at, though perhaps it has rarely been known that so firm and lasting a friendship, **for I must so call it,** has been so suddenly contracted.

Whatever Lady Masham felt she "must" call the relationship—not *necessarily* because of the grim penalties of buggery laws at the time—it certainly was a "firm" relationship made in nearly a heartbeat (even if a fluttering one). Shortly after the initial meeting, Locke had several cozy dinners in Oxford with Shaftesbury (no pun intended by the name, but perhaps unavoidable), and, according to Bourne, the two men very soon traveled away from Oxford, to Sunninghill—a small out-of-the-way village outside of London—where Locke "spent the first fortnight [two weeks] of August with Lord Ashley." In the spring of the following year, Locke went and visited Lord Ashley again, "at Wimborne St. Giles's, his country house in Dorsetshire." After a few more months, on 15 June 1667, Locke took up permanent residence at "Exeter House, the London residence of Lord Ashley," where Locke lived, according to Lady Masham, "with my Lord Ashley as a man at home." Indeed.

There is an always entertaining reference work, Alexander Chalmers's *General Biographical Dictionary* of 1812, which begins its entry on Lord Ashley this way: "Cooper, Anthony Ashley, earl of Shaftesbury, an eminent statesman of very dubious character." Expanding on that, the entry offers:

It was also a standing jest with the lower form of wits, to style him Shiftsbury instead of Shaftesbury. The author who relates this, tells us also, that when he was chancellor, one sir Paul Neal watered his mares with rhenish and sugar: that is, entertained his mistresses. In his female connections he was very licentious; and it is recorded, that Charles II, who would both take liberties and bear them, once said to the earl at court, in a vein of raillery and good humour, and in reference only to his amours, "I believe, Shaftesbury, thou art the wickedest fellow in my dominions:" to which, with a low bow and very grave face, the earl replied, "May it please your majesty, of a subject I believe I am;" at which the merry monarch laughed heartily.

Whether Ashley's licentiousness extended beyond "female connections" is left only to speculation, but such speculation needn't be very elastic. There is another form of "eulogy" that was written about Shaftesbury in 1685, within a few years after his 1683 death. It was written by someone who had allowed Shaftesbury to get very close indeed, and who—as we already have seen, and soon will see more of—had granted to Shaftesbury quite a few honors, along with property, wealth, and power. Shaftesbury, for thanks, had plotted to have this person and his brother assassinated. That person was King Charles II, king of the three kingdoms of England, Scotland, and Ireland. A very detailed account of the murderous plot that Shaftesbury masterminded was published in 1685 with the magisterial title of *A True Account and Declaration of the Horrid Conspiracy Against the Late King, His Present Majesty, and the Government*, printed by Thomas Newcomb. It is the exact account that King Charles II wanted printed, and had approved of just before his own death. In it he had this to say, among other things, about the treachery of Shaftesbury (capitalization, punctuation, and spelling as in the original):

> This was indeed a Talent peculiar to the Earl of Shaftsbury [sic], That of all Men living he could most easily turn himself into all shapes, and comply with all Dispositions ; having by long practice, got the skill to cover his Hooks with Baits fitting every Humour. The Covetous who are no small Number of the pretended Godly Party, those he was wont to feed, and deceive with hopes of Wealth and new Sequestrations : The Ambitious with Praise and Vain-Glory: The Nonconformist Zealots, with Promises of Liberty in Religion ; sometimes not refusing to stoop lower, and even to serve and assist the Pleasures and Debauches of Men that way inclined, if he found them any way useful for his purpose.

The phrase "to serve and assist the Pleasures and Debauches of *Men that way inclined*" should leave little doubt about the intended meaning, at least to those not predisposed to worshipping Shaftesbury and Locke. Lord Ashley/Shaftesbury had a wife and several children—but then, so had Mervyn Tuchet, 2nd Earl of Castlehaven, who had lost his head (literally) for having fiddled (not literally) with his page, Laurence FitzPatrick.

As for Locke: People in polite company might have referred to John Locke as a "confirmed bachelor." A churchman at Oxford who had more than a few encounters with Locke, Humphrey Prideaux, once described Locke's relationship with a man named Robert West—who later would end up being among the conspirators in Shaftesbury's plot to kill the king. When news of West's arrest for that plot made its way to Oxford, where Locke was at the time:

> He [John Locke] was very solicitous to know of us at the table who this West

was; at which one made an unlucky reply, that it was the very same person whom he [Locke] treated at his chambers and caressed at so great a rate ... here at Oxford; which put the gentleman [Locke] into a profound silence, and the next thing we heard of him was that he was fled for the same.

Locke soon afterward fled to Holland. All of this gets ahead in the story, but it's important to have these insights into Locke's nature and "character," if that word can be so basely employed.

Many of Locke's biographers make the downright silly claim that Ashley took Locke into his bosom and home as a "personal physician." Nonsense. Here Locke was such a laggard that he had failed to meet the qualifications for a degree in medicine, and Ashley had to go calling in favors at the king's court just to allow Locke to go on being a student (which Locke then shirked some more). Shaftesbury could have had any of the finest physicians in England, so to claim that he clutched onto Locke for that purpose is simply laughable, and another way that Locke's fanboy disciples have tried to polish Locke's halo. While it's true that Locke ultimately performed a unique, if relatively minor, surgical opening in Shaftesbury's abdomen to allow for drainage of an internal abscess through a silver tube—credited with having saved Shaftesbury's life—even that was done with the counsel and concurrence of no fewer than five doctors, four of them described by Bourne as "the most famous physicians of the day."

Almost equally silly are the abundant assertions that Locke was Ashley/Shaftsbury's "secretary." Although there's no question that Locke performed some personal secretarial duties for Ashley/ Shaftesbury, and a great deal of business-related secretarial duties having to do with the colonies and slave trading, Locke had great latitude in what he did or didn't do at any given time. A man named Thomas Stringer has been nearly eclipsed from history by the dazzle of Lockean mythology, but was a very important companion to Ashley/Shaftesbury, and Bourne even describes Stringer specifically as "Lord Shaftesbury's secretary" as of 1672. We'll meet Stringer again in several places in this narrative.

For now, this is merely a brief first glimpse at "the man behind the curtain," John Locke, looming larger than any Wizard of Oz or any wizard anywhere over every man, woman, and child on this planet.

This is the man to whom, if you buy his carnival barking, you—yes, you, reader—are "equal."

This is the materialist, atheist, and shameless opportunist who would have you accept without question that Martin Luther King is equal to Martin Luther and that both are equal to Adolf Hitler. Mother Theresa is not one bit different from Osama bin Laden. And Thomas Jefferson is nothing more nor less than Karl Marx in powdered hair. No, they can't be any different from each other, because we all are "equal."

John Locke was the miserably mortal "maker" of a fictional "Maker" that supposedly created all men "equal"—and Locke has been worshipped as though a god himself ever since by people who should know better, many of them applauded materialists, many of them displaying framed dusty degrees from alleged institutions of "higher learning." In upcoming trips through the Lockean tar, we're going to encounter more than a few of them, struggling and fighting each other in the sticky mess. Just one example of Locke's hallowed status, out of countless others available, comes from Philip Abrams, described in his 1967 book on John Locke's *Two Tracts on Government* as "Fellow of Peterhouse and lecturer in Economics and Politics in the University of Cambridge." Abrams called Locke "the presiding genius of liberal democracy."

The only assumption that can be made is that the good Dr. Abrams didn't subscribe to Locke's decree that we all are "created equal;" if he did, there couldn't be a "presiding genius."

If there was genius in Locke, it reflected the "genius" attributed to his mentor—and possibly lover—Shaftesbury: it was genius in duplicity, in cunning manipulation, in hypocrisy, in double-talk, and, as we'll soon see, in "borrowing" the work of others and selling it as his own. He was a sycophantic charmer. He charmed the pants off—so to speak—Lord Shaftesbury, or this book would not exist, because Shaftesbury subsidized the idleness that allowed Locke to drown the world in tedious tar.

No matter what the intimate details of the relationship between

Locke and Shaftesbury, it is a bet-the-farm certainty that Lord Shaftesbury pulled the strings in November 1666 that rescued Locke from the clawing clutches of clergydom—less than 90 days after Locke and Shaftesbury had spent two weeks together in Sunninghill. In doing so, Shaftesbury shafted us all, condemning the world to the ravings of a madman.

And what ravings they are.

5. "Equal and Independent"—Deranged Twins of Lockean Lunacy
The Delirious Duo

It's a wonder that someone didn't have John Locke put into restraints and goat-carted to Bedlam the instant he first babbled that mankind was all "equal and independent." "Equal" and "Independent" are like the Tweedledum and Tweedledee of philosophy, pointing in different directions—and even twins aren't "equal," either. The two conditions are mutually exclusive, and the claim of "independence" is every bit as deranged as the claim of "equality"—yet today Locke's mad and muddled musings seem almost mundane, so pervasively have they been ground in as permanent stains on the social fabric.

Apologists for Locke and for his many "equality" disciples—Jefferson being only one in a flock of such disciples—will cheerfully waste hours, days, or even years of your time insisting, demanding, pounding on desks to convince you that Locke and friends only ever meant "equality under the law"—meaning under *civil* law, the laws of polities and governments. Grade school teachers and high school teachers all over the world stand in front of impressionable children every day the sun shines and tell that blatant lie to those children. It is false on its face. Locke's dogma was based *entirely* on his perverse proposition that all men were "equal and independent" in the "State of Nature" and under the "Law of Nature"—*before there were any man-made laws.* That is so plain, clear, and inarguable that you would think that the dopiest of halfwits could understand it—even though

49

teachers and professors apparently don't:

> The State of Nature has a Law of Nature to govern it, which obliges every one: And Reason, which is that Law, teaches all Mankind who will but consult it, that being all equal and independent, no one ought to harm another in his Life, Health, Liberty or Possession. —**John Locke,** *Second Treatise on Government*

Of course, Locke conveniently never got around to telling anybody exactly what this "state of nature" or the "laws of nature" were (about which more later), but *all* of his gibbering—*all of it*—was built on this nebulous, undefined, self-contradictory, and nonexistent "foundation" of some imaginary fantasy world that no preschool child would fall for, where every single person in it is entirely "equal and independent."

The nearly unimaginable reality that somehow must be grasped is that there is *not a scrap of foundation* for *any* of Locke's endless whims, stacked like yesterday's tea cups, topped off with a teetering non sequitur pronouncement, worthy of the Mad Hatter, that all men are "equal and independent." The Lockean proclamations all float above a nonexistent floor in midair.

What "Equality"? The Hyper-Hypocrisy of "Created Equal"

Even though Thomas Jefferson forwarded the *equality* dogma from Locke's words and theories, Jefferson didn't believe that "all men are created equal." He knew very well that they weren't—and said as much. Some of Jefferson's correspondence is preserved in a praiseworthy collection of historic documents, published originally in a five-volume anthology called *The Founders' Constitution,* now available on the Internet as a joint venture of the University of Chicago Press and the Liberty Fund. It is owed an homage for its documents, but not necessarily for its sometimes turgidly inscrutable exposition, such as this brief observation by its editors about Jefferson and "equality":

> Jefferson's [19 July 1778] letter to David Rittenhouse on the inequality of talents ... makes an extraordinary gloss on the opening paragraph of the Declaration.

"Gloss"? That description by the editors of The Founders' Constitution is a gloss on a gloss, because in reading Jefferson's actual words from his letter to the astronomer Rittenhouse, the word "mockery" comes more to mind:

> Nobody can conceive that nature ever intended to throw away a Newton upon the occupations of a crown. It would have been a prodigality for which even the conduct of providence might have been arraigned, had he been by birth annexed to what was so far below him. Cooperating with nature in her ordinary economy, we should dispose of and employ the geniuses of men according to their several orders and degrees. —*Thomas Jefferson to David Rittenhouse, 19 July 1778*

That letter was written by Jefferson two years after the same man unabashedly had written "all men are created equal" in the *Declaration of Independence,* altering the course of history. But Jefferson didn't stop with Rittenhouse. In a letter of 28 October 1813 to John Adams, Jefferson doubled down—forcefully:

> I agree with you that there is a natural aristocracy among men. The grounds of this are virtue and talents. Formerly bodily powers gave place among the aristoi [word for noblemen in ancient Greece]. But since the invention of gunpowder has armed the weak as well as the strong with missile death, bodily strength, like beauty, good humor, politeness and other accomplishments, has become but an auxiliary ground of distinction.
>
> There is also an artificial aristocracy founded on wealth and birth, without either virtue or talents; for with these it would belong to the first class.
>
> The natural aristocracy I consider as the most precious gift of nature for the instruction, the trusts, and government of society. And indeed it would have been inconsistent in creation to have formed man for the social state, and not to have provided virtue and wisdom enough to manage the concerns of the society. May we not even say that that form of government is the best which provides the most effectually for a pure selection of these natural aristoi into the offices of government?
>
> The artificial aristocracy is a mischievous ingredient in government, and provision should be made to prevent it's ascendancy. —*Thomas Jefferson to John Adams, 28 October 1813*

So much for "created equal." The very fact that Jefferson himself owned slaves at the time, and throughout his life, should have been a clanging clue to the cognitive dissonance being writ large in the phrase "all men are created equal."

But if Jefferson's multi-tracked view on alleged "equality"

amongst human beings seems even slightly hypocritical, it is nothing but a whiff in the wind compared with the hurricane of hypocrisy from the blowhard John Locke. Iris Därmann, a German cultural scientist and philosopher who served as professor of cultural sciences at Humboldt University of Berlin, summed it up succinctly in her 2014 article "Myths of Labor" for a German journal:

> Locke succeeded through share purchases in the Royal African Company (RAC) and Bahama Adventures, founded in 1672, in gaining significant profits from the transatlantic slave trade. ... In the decree written by him of the Fundamental Constitutions of Carolina it is stated that every free man "shall have absolute power and authority over his Negro slaves." This corresponds in turn to the Instructions of Governor Francis Nicholson of Virginia which Locke helped to draft in 1698. These viewed every Negro slave as legally enslaved who had been captured in a "just war" and thus forfeited his life through an act worthy of the death penalty.

Author John Tully, in *An Approach to Political Philosophy: Locke in Contexts,* wrote:

> Locke was one of the six or eight men who ... helped to shape the old colonial system during the Restoration. He invested in the slave-trading Royal Africa Company [sic: Royal African Company] (1671) and the Company of Merchant Adventurers to trade with the Bahamas (1672).

What neither of those accounts above reveals is Locke's opportunistic in-the-woodwork plotting to create and sustain both the demand and the logistics for his profiteering from slave trading. He did it through—and you might have guessed—Lord Ashley/Shaftesbury. Only a timeline can reveal the fullness of Locke's cunning, self-serving duplicity.

Before getting to any such timeline, it must be mentioned that the various second-hand accounts of the "Royal African Company"— or sometimes even, incorrectly, "Royal *Africa* Company," as in Tully above—and its relationship to the names "Company of Royal Adventurers *into* Africa," or "Company of Royal Adventurers *in* Africa," or "Company of Royal Adventurers of England trading into Africa," or "Company of Royal Adventurers Trading *to* Africa," or "Company of Royal Adventurers trading *into* Africa" (and even other weird variations) is a hedge maze of history that few ever have emerged from. There is a bewildering inconsistency of names in the various second-hand accounts of these companies. Except where quoting second-hand "experts," as above, I will use, going forward, the names found in *actual historical records,* mostly taken from a marvelous book published in 1913 by the Seldon Society of London, edited by Cecil T. Carr: *Select Charters of Trading Companies, A. D. 1530–1707.* It contains the texts of the kingly charters that established those companies, correctly dated, so those company names and dates are correctly and faithfully recorded in the timeline below.

A similar confusion arises with the name of another company, which has variously been called (or miscalled) in the literature "Company of Merchant Adventurers to trade with the Bahamas," or "Bahama Adventures," or "Bahama Adventurers," or "Adventurers to Bahamas." It is hoped that merely calling attention to this name-game will untangle the confusion for the timeline below that relevantly includes John Locke. The timeline will state the information about the company correctly, as taken from the appropriate records.

As though that weren't enough to contend with, there is a similar regrettable confusion among many history "experts" surrounding the names of various councils responsible at different times for overseeing England's trade, or its foreign plantations, or both. I have found no more competently detailed an authority on this mess than Charles M. Andrews, in his 1908 work, *British Committees, Commissions, and Councils of Trade and Plantations, 1622–1675.* In the timeline below, I rely heavily on his dogged detective work in sorting out these sometimes foggily defined groups, in conjunction with records available from British History Online.

With those caveats, here is a timeline of relevant events, all of them building toward Locke becoming a major investor in the most debased greed at all—human trafficking. The timeline, of necessity, begins with matters involving Ashley/Shaftesbury:

7 November 1660

King Charles II creates a **Council of Trade.** Quoted from Andrews: "The commission for the Council of Trade passed the great seal on that day and is dated November 7, 1660." Anthony Ashley Cooper—later Lord Ashley/Lord Shaftesbury—is part of this Council of Trade.

1 December 1660
King Charles II appoints the first **Council of Foreign Plantations** under his reign, consisting of 49 commissioners—one of which is Sir Anthony Ashley Cooper (later Lord Ashley/Lord Shaftesbury), listed in the appointment as "Cooper, Sir A. A." Also among the commissioners are Edward Hyde (later Lord Clarendon), and William Morice, the king's Secretary of State for the Northern Department. (There will be a *second* Council of Foreign Plantations appointed by Charles II at a later date, a fact that has tripped up some historians.)

It is of crucial interest to interject here that there was a good deal of overlap in the membership of these two *different* "councils" created in 1660—the Council of Trade, and the separate Council of Foreign Plantations. This likely has contributed to the swirling confusion in the existing "expert" literature on the subject, but the main takeaway for this timeline is that Sir Anthony Ashley Cooper was a member of *both*: the Council of Trade *and* the Council of Foreign Plantations. Also straddling both councils were Lord Clarendon and Sir William Morice—each of whom will eventually write special letters on behalf of John Locke.

18 December 1660
King Charles II issues "Letters Patent" that incorporate **The Company of the Royal Adventurers into Africa** [exact formal name from the document]. The Letters Patent simultaneously grant to that corporation almost the entire west coast of Africa for colonizing and trade. This gives the company an English monopoly on gold and other valued commodities from the region. The management of

the company is left to six "agents"—but King Charles II's brother James, the Duke of York, is the Lord High Admiral of England, and by some accounts is the de facto director of the company. [NOTE: Within the same document, the company is referred to simply as the **Company of Royal Adventurers into Africa.** This duality of naming in the founding document has probably contributed to some of the confusion, with this less wordy and more informal name catching on—and sometimes even that misstated.]

20 April 1661
Anthony Ashley Cooper is created Cooper Baron Ashley, of Wimborne St. Giles—or, more simply, Lord Ashley—by King Charles II. This allows Ashley to serve in the House of Lords.

13 May 1661
Lord Ashley is appointed as Chancellor of the Exchequer of England, under King Charles II. It is one of four Great Offices of State. He replaces Edward Hyde—Lord Clarendon—who continues in his other role as Chief Minister of England, and who is Lord Ashley's "recognized chief" (Bourne). Lord Clarendon's daughter, Anne Hyde, is married to James, Duke of York, who is the brother of Charles II, and who essentially holds the English monopoly on African trading—including Negro slaves.

10 January 1663
King Charles II issues a charter that supplants the "Letters Patents" of 18 December 1660 (see above). The grant creates a new company with a somewhat different, if similar, name: **The Company of Royal Adventurers of England Trading into Africa.** The charter grants to this newly formed company essentially the same swath of the west coast of Africa that had been granted to the first such company, and all trading rights there, including "any red wood, elephants'

teeth, Negro slaves, hides, wax, gums, grains," or other commodities, as well as all rights to gold and silver mines (a respectable share going, of course, to the crown). The king's brother, James, Duke of York, is the de facto manager, given the power to call a meeting to elect a governor and other officers of the company. [NOTE: This document, like its predecessor of 18 December 1660, makes mention in the text, somewhat ambiguously, of the **Company of Royal Adventurers into Africa.** It's impossible to tell from the context whether that refers to the earlier company, or to the one just formed, and this, also, likely has contributed to the confusion by some "experts."]

This incorporation expressly grants to this company a British monopoly on the slave trade being facilitated at the time by indigenous African Negro tribes, such as the Yoruba and Akans, who were capturing and selling Negro slaves to the European colonists and traders. George Frederick Zook expands on this aspect of the new company's interests in his 1919 book, *The Company of Royal Adventurers Trading Into Africa* (all punctuation, or lack thereof, from original):

> The new charter contained the same provisions in regard to the discovery of gold mines as the charter of 1660. By this time, however, the adventurers had discovered that the Negro trade could be made very lucrative. In this charter, therefore, they obtained "the whole, entire and only trade for the buying and selling bartering and exchanging of for or with any Negroes, slaves, goods, wares and merchandises whatsoever to be vented or found at or within any of the Cities" on the west coast of Africa. The charter provided that there should be no trading on the African coast except by the company in its corporate capacity, and that any one guilty of transgressing these rules should be liable to forfeiture of his ship and goods.
>
> The charter also required the shareholders to elect a governor, subgovernor, deputy governor and court of assistants; but that the routine business of the company should be conducted by a smaller committee corresponding to the committee of six of the previous company. The Duke of York [the king's brother] was elected governor, in which capacity he continued to serve during the company's entire existence.

Back to the timeline, as Ashley increases his power and fortune—and meets John Locke:

24 March 1663

King Charles II issues a charter that grants dominion over a large tract of land in America to eight "Lords Proprietors." The land—formerly called the Province of Carolana—becomes known as Carolina, and the Lords Proprietors are the ruling landlords, charged with developing the colonies and plantations there. Among the eight Lords Proprietors are Lord Ashley and Lord Clarendon—both of whom are also on the first Council of Foreign Plantations, and on the Council of Trade.

20 c. July 1666

Lord Ashley travels to Oxford for the allegedly healing waters. There he has his first encounter with John Locke, and they soon go off for two weeks together in a country village.

This provides now some relevant context for Locke's meeting with Lord Ashley, and for the scope of Ashley's power, wealth, and influence at the time. Although Ashley was not directly involved with The Company of Royal Adventurers of England Trading into Africa, he was a member of both the Council of Trade and the Council of Foreign Plantations, so he was well aware indeed of the nascent transatlantic slave trade, and of the growing demand for slaves in the English colonies and plantations, including in the American territories he now owned a significant part of. Not long after he and Locke met and spent their two private weeks together:

3 November 1666

Lord Clarendon writes an extraordinary letter on behalf of John Locke to keep him from having to go into the clergy, urging the administrators at Christ Church, Oxford, to allow him to maintain his student status there. There can be no other explanation than that Lord Ashley influenced Clarendon on Locke's behalf. The letter, though, doesn't convince the administrators of the school to grant Locke the special status.

14 November 1666

After Clarendon's letter fails, William Morice, King Charles II's Secretary of State for the Northern Department, writes a royal "dispensation" for Locke to be allowed to continue his student status. It sticks. (Note that Clarendon and Ashley are both Lords Proprietors of Carolina; that Morice, Clarendon, and Ashley are all commissioners of the first Council of Foreign Plantations; and that all three hold high offices in the king's ministry. It is absurd to think that Morice and Clarendon would have thrown their weight for Locke without Ashley's personal intervention.)

15 June 1667

John Locke takes up residence with Lord Ashley and his family at Ashley's London home, Exeter House. Whatever else he's doing, Locke soon becomes "in some sort of irregular way the chief secretary or manager of the whole company of Lords Proprietors of Carolina" because Ashley is "the most active and influential" of the Lords Proprietors (Bourne). It is around this same time that Locke pens his first draft of the work that later would become known—mostly—as "An **Essay** Concerning Toleration." [NOTE: This should not be confused with Locke's first *published* work, published during his lifetime, which is called—mostly—"A **Letter** Concerning Toleration," sometimes called "A **Letter** on Toleration," and which was originally written in Latin as *Epistola de Tolerantia*. Now you probably are confused. Don't feel bad: so are many of the "experts." In any case, Locke's "An **Essay** Concerning Toleration" went through four different drafts, and many of the concepts ended up in the first-published work, "A **Letter** Concerning Toleration." The various versions of "An **Essay** Concerning Toleration" were not published until the 18th century, long after Locke's death.]

There's certainly more to this timeline leading to Locke's direct investment in African slavery, but it must be interjected here that the *Shaftesbury Papers* provide considerable insights into Locke's activities after he took up residence with Ashley/Shaftesbury. Bourne's biography of Locke sums up one crucial aspect of Locke's access to and involvement in the business of the colony of Carolina—which included the slave trade for the plantations being established there:

> Down to the autumn of 1672 [Locke] continued his informal, but onerous, office of secretary to the Proprietors, and the documents that are extant throw much light on his occupations at this time. Nearly every letter received from the colony is docqueted by him, and of a great number of letters that have disappeared there exist careful epitomes in his handwriting. We have also drafts, entered by him, of numerous letters sent out from England, and his hand is plainly shown in other letters. Out of these materials it would be easy to construct almost the entire history of the colony [Carolina] during the first years of its existence.

There are no accurate records to be found of the number of slaves being transported to the Carolinas during this period, but many of the slaves bound for there, and for other parts of North America, came through the Bahama Islands—which themselves soon would be in the control of Ashley/Shaftesbury and Locke. One undated record in the 1668 collection of *Colonial State Papers, West Indies* of England's Public Records Office is "A short computation of expense in settling and improving the Bahama Islands." The document is estimated to have been created in 1667, certainly by 1668, the very time period of Locke's initial intense involvement. Among the items listed are the following:

> 600 slaves at 30£ each: £18,000

> It is proposed to trade for 4,000 negroes per annum, being 8,000 for the first two years (before any returns can be expected) at 25£ per head, delivered at [New] Providence [Bahamas]: £200,000

With that context, the timeline continues:

15 c. April 1669

The Lords Proprietors chip in £500 apiece for an expedition to North America to start establishing colonies in the Carolinas. Lord Ashley's Exeter House in London is headquarters for the operation, and Locke is its "principle superintendent" (Bourne).

21 July 1669

John Locke writes "The Fundamental Constitutions for the Government of Carolina" in his own hand. It will not be formally approved and issued by the Lords Proprietors until 1 March of the following year, with only a few changes from Locke's first draft. In it, Locke puts the following provisions:

> No slave shall hereby be exempted from that civil dominion his master hath over him, but be in all things in the same state and condition he was In before. ... Every freeman of Carolina shall have absolute power and authority over his negro slaves.

In addition to the official sanctioning of slaves, Locke also creates a class of servants, or, essentially, serfs, which he calls "leet-men" and "leet-women," who are to be under complete domination of their land-owning "lords."

22 January 1670

A report from Jamaica provides some indication of the demand for slaves in the New World at the time. Out of a reported total population of 8,200, there are 2,500 "negroes or slaves," almost a third of the population.

["America and West Indies: January 1670," in Calendar of State Papers Colonial, America and West Indies: Volume 7, 1669-1674, ed. W Noel Sainsbury (London: Her Majesty's Stationery Office, 1889), 49-55. British History Online, accessed November 2, 2017, http://www.british-history. ac.uk/cal-state-papers/colonial/america-west-indies/vol7/ pp49-55.]

17 February 1670

A petition is sent by "John Dorrell senior, and Hugh Wentworth"—two pioneering inhabitants of New Providence, Bahamas—to Lord Ashley, "examined by John Locke," requesting that Ashley use his influence "by gaining a patent for all the Bahama Islands so they may be governed according to His Majesty's laws, and that themselves may be remembered as the first beginners and encouragers of the settlement of New Providence." [NOTE: It won't be long before Ashley finagles just such a "patent" of ownership for the Bahamas—but for himself and his friends, not for the petitioners.] A little over a week after the petition ...

1 March 1670

The Fundamental Constitutions for the Government of Carolina—written in John Locke's hand—are officially adopted by the Lords Proprietors. It creates a new pyramid of hereditary "nobility" for that part of America, using titles Locke made up or "borrowed" from other cultures. Not surprisingly, the Lords Proprietors are at the top of the social order, holding "seigniories," with the most land. The eldest of their number is titled the "Palatine." Below them are "baronies," based on land ownership, as granted by the Lords Proprietors.

Locke's scheme of aristocracy for the Carolinas was so complex and fuzzily stated that every "expert" who tries to describe it seems to come up with something different, but the aristocratic titles laid out in the Carolina constitution included Landgraves, Caziques (or Casiques), and Baronets, the pecking order based on land holdings. At the bottom of the Lockean pyramid were servants—called "leet-men"—and slaves. The line between leet-men and slaves was not very clearly drawn, given these mandates in the constitution:

> In every signiory, barony, and manor, all the leet-men shall be under the

jurisdiction of the respective lords of the said signiory, barony, or manor, without appeal from him. Nor shall any leet-man or leet-woman have liberty to go off from the land of their particular lord and live anywhere else, without license obtained from their said lord, under hand and seal.

All the children of leet-men shall be leet-men, and so to all generations.

And, yes: this hierarchy of totalitarian hereditary aristocracy, complete with servants and slaves, came from John Locke—poster boy for every liberal college and university currently peddling his propaganda—who soon would be preaching to the world how we're all supposedly "equal and independent." Before he got around to that, though, he arranged to get himself nicely set up in his own newly created aristocracy—and in the transatlantic slave trade:

30 July 1670

As a result of Ashley-Shaftesbury's machinations, a *new* Council of Foreign Plantations is created by King Charles II. Lord Ashley is part of it because he is Chancellor of the Exchequer, and some commissioners are added who receive a salary—"payable at the Exchequer." This gives Ashley considerable leverage over them all, even though the Earl of Sandwich is the titular president of the council. And just about 90 days later ...

1 November 1670

King Charles II officially grants to Lord Ashley and the other Lords Proprietors of Carolina "all those islands called Bahama, Eleutheria, Ucanis (?) [sic], [New] Providence, Inagua, and all other those islands lying in the degrees of 22 to 27 north lat., commonly known by the name of the Bahama Islands, or the Islands of the Lucayos." This provides the Lords Proprietors with enormous power over the buying, selling, and transportation of African slaves bound for the Bahamas or the mainland colonies.

1 May 1671

The Lords Proprietors send "Carolina Instructions," laying out steps to create a Parliament and a Grand Council there, along with other mandates. One of those instructions is: "To set out baronies according to the Fundamental Constitutions to James Carteret, Sir John Yeamans, and John Locke, who have been made landgraves." According to Harvard University's David Armitage, Locke's "landgrave" title came with 48,000 acres. ("John Locke: Theorist of Empire?" http://nrs.harvard.edu/urn-3:HUL.InstRepos:10718367)

6 April 1671

In the House of Lords Journal Volume 12:6 of this date, there is a "Royal African Company Bill," described as: "An Act for incorporating the Company of Royal Adventurers of England trading into Africa." [NOTE: This is one place where the informal shorthand name "Royal African Company" becomes conflated with the name "Company of Royal Adventurers of England trading into Africa." There is not yet, though, anything *officially* named, *specifically*, the "Royal African Company," and won't be until 27 September 1672. Also, George F. Zook says of this bill: "In April ... a bill had been introduced into the House of Lords to incorporate the company by act of Parliament. On account of the various plans under consideration there was no procedure with the bill." —Ed.]

15 c. June 1671

At Exeter House in London, John Locke submits a report to the Lords Proprietors saying that fellow landgrave Sir John Yeamans, believing he is to become the new governor of Carolina, has arrived in Carolina from Barbados. Part of Locke's report says, "He has brought negroes and expects more." According to Henry William Elston's *History of the United States,* Yeamans has brought with him "about two hundred African slaves."

11 July 1671

Date of the first draft of John Locke's *Essay Concerning Human Understanding*. It will not be published until 1689, with some portion of it having been "printed in 1688," apparently for limited distribution. It is in this essay that Locke proposes that man is simply a category of animal, without innate knowledge, or ethics, or soul, whose knowledge, identity, and essence consists entirely and only of material sensory impressions from the external world. [Perhaps this helped assuage Locke's conscience, if he had any, for trading humans as chattel. —Ed.]

28 October 1671

The Company of Royal Adventurers of England trading into Africa has not been faring well due to various wars and conflicts, and is heavily in debt. On this date the "preamble and articles" for a "new subscription" (shares for investors) are royally approved, with notice to the existing creditors that they must accept a partial payment arrangement within 10 days, or "the king would revoke the company's patent." (Zook) [NOTE: This is the beginning of the new royal company, which eventually will be named, officially, the "New Royal African Company." —Ed.]

10 January 1672

A "general court" of the new subscribers to the Company of Royal Adventurers of England trading into Africa is held, electing James, Duke of York, as the governor, with Lord Ashley elected to subgovernor (Zook). At or around this time, John Locke buys either £400 of £600 worth of shares in this newly forming company. (Depends on who you listen to.) The £400 amount happens to be the minimum investment necessary for eligibility to become an officer in the company.

23 April 1672

Lord Ashley is "raised to the peerage as Earl of Shaftesbury" (Bourne).

30 April 1672

Almost immediately after Lord Ashley's promotion to Earl of Shaftesbury, instructions are written for one "William Lord Willoughby, Governor of Barbadoes," who is leaving for the islands to take control. Part of those instructions include: "Encouragement to be given to merchants, and in particular to the Royal African Company, taking care that payment be duly made them according to agreements; an account from time to time to be given to his Majesty and the Council for Plantations of negroes yearly supplied to the islands, and at what rates."["America and West Indies: April 1672," in Calendar of State Papers Colonial, America and West Indies: Volume 7, 1669-1674, ed. W Noel Sainsbury (London: Her Majesty's Stationery Office, 1889), 344-354. British History Online, accessed November 2, 2017, http://www.british-history.ac.uk/cal-state-papers/colonial/america-west-indies/vol7/pp344-354.] [NOTE: Here again the rather informal use of the name "Royal African Company" is being used to refer to the "Company of Royal Adventurers of England trading into Africa." It is likely that Lord Shaftesbury and the other insiders know that the new company replacing the old is going to be called the "New Royal African Company." —Ed.]

Within a few months, things began to happen rapidly in the month of September 1672, and it's impossible to escape the conclusion that Shaftesbury's insider knowledge of all things having to do with trade, slaves, plantations, and colonies, especially in the Bahamas and Carolina, where he had ownership interests, put him and Locke in very fortuitous circumstances.

4 September 1672

The Lords Proprietors of Carolina—including, of course, Shaftesbury—enter into an agreement with 11 investors, called the "Adventurers to Bahamas," for them to purchase 12,000 acres in New Providence, Bahamas, for £1,600, and to purchase "as much in any other of the islands that they chose." John Locke—already an investor in the newly forming company that will be named the New Royal African Company—invests an initial £100 as an "Adventurer to Bahamas." Another of the investors is Thomas Stringer, described as "Lord Shaftesbury's secretary" (Bourne). [NOTE: Whereas Bourne uses the name "Adventurers to Bahamas," Armitage cites a record of the Hampshire Record Office, Winchester, Malmesbury Papers, with the name "Articles of Agreement of the Bahamas Adventurers." Take your pick. —Ed.]

16 September 1672

England's Attorney General is instructed to prepare a bill for King Charles II to sign, which will reorganize the Council of Trade and the Council of Foreign Plantations into one council, called formally the "Council for all Affairs relating to Trade and Foreign Colonies and Plantations." Its name will end up being simply the Council of Trade and Foreign Plantations. Lord Shaftesbury is listed to be one of the council members.

21 September 1672

For no apparent reason, John Locke departs London for Paris. He is accompanied by a friend and fellow investor in the Bahama Adventurers, John Mapletoft.

27 September 1672

A momentous day. The king signs and seals the creation of the Council of Trade and Foreign Plantations. Lord

Shaftesbury is named as president of the council. On the same day, the king creates by the Great Seal the Charter of Incorporation of the New Royal African Company. James, Duke of York, is named as governor, with Lord Shaftesbury as subgovernor. John Locke is named in the charter, being among the primary investors

23 October 1672
John Locke has returned from his short trip to France. At a meeting of the Bahamas Adventurers, he doubles his investment by receiving a transfer of £100 worth of shares from his friend John Mapletoft, who has remained in France.

There it is. It is inarguable. John Locke—the secularly sanctified source of the entire insane "equal and independent" dogma—was a major, primary, founding investor in the giant Royal African Company slave-trading profiteers, which in just 17 years, from 1672 through 1689, bought and sold at least 90,000 slaves, possibly as many as 100,000, according to best estimates. Many of those slaves were branded with the initials RAC to mark them as the company's property. John Locke was a major force in creation of the transatlantic African slave trade that roared on under RAC and others for well over a century. John Locke knowingly, willfully used his connections and insider knowledge to get himself well invested in the new colonies and in the trading of slaves to develop those colonies for himself and his cronies.

According to Peter Laslett's thoroughgoing analysis and speculation in his book *John Locke: Two Treatises of Government*, it was during the years 1679 to 1683—while Locke mostly was living comfortably in London, Oxford, and Oakley, enjoying the profits of his investments in the misery and enslavement of tens of thousands of human beings—that he wrote *Two Treatises on Government*, in which he haughtily declared that all men were "equal and independent." And it was in 1685, after he had profited from actively supporting the most inhumane degradations and deaths of human beings as slaves, that he flipped up his coattails, sat down, and sanctimoniously penned the published version of his "A **Letter** Concerning Toleration."

Yet this slave-trading hypocrite, Locke, is all but knelt down to as the Lord High Priest and Grand High Wizard of "equality" and "tolerance" by every progressive, globalist, liberal, leftist, like-minded lunatic on earth—and by most conservatives. That dichotomy ought to be a wake-up bucket of cold water in the face. As a result, the poisonous propaganda of his hyperbolic hypocrisy is preached in every grade school, high school, college, and university in the world.

For all its art and power, the English language sits down and gives up in any attempt to adequately describe the depravity of John Locke's holier-than-thou hypocrisy.

There's no way of knowing exactly what was going through Jefferson's mind as he sat composing his draft in the Graff house— we hope romantically lit by candles, with the scritch and scratch of a feather pen—when his hand moved in fluid cursive motion to write out the opening words of the *Declaration of Independence*. If he was trying to say that all men should have equal rights under the law, or equal freedoms, or equal justice—as so many "equality" dictators try to claim—he did a miserably poor job of it. [For extensive discussion of "rights under the law" arguments, see chapters 9 through 13 —Ed.] Instead, he penned the most generalized and mortifyingly unqualified statement imaginable: "all men are created equal." It's bad enough that it was so egregiously broad, and that it has been taken literally by so many of the not-very-bright squad, but even worse is that the statement is false on its face, and falls on its face.

Baldly put, it's a lie. It is the greatest lie.

Locke's "equal" madness is nearly matched by his "independent" madness.

"Equal and Independent"? What "Independence"?

No human being ever has come into this life being anything but utterly *dependent* on two parents for the *very fact of existence,* and utterly *dependent* on at least one parent to nurse and nurture its every need, including all sustenance and locomotion.

John Locke, in his endless worminess in words, tried desperately, pathetically, to address this fatal flaw of his "equal and independent" dogma in his *Second Treatise on Government*:

> Though I have said above ... "That all men by nature are equal" ... Children, I confess, are not born in this state of equality, though they are born to it. Their parents have a sort of rule and jurisdiction over them, when they come into the world, and for some time after; but it is but a temporary one.

Are you laughing yet? If not, get your pulse checked. And then within mere paragraphs, Locke (again) contradicts himself, tying himself in knots attempting to escape his own self-contradictions:

> Thus we are born free, as we are born rational; not that we have actually the exercise of either: age, that brings one, brings with it the other too. And thus we see how natural freedom and subjection to parents may consist together, and are both founded on the same principle. A child is free by his father's title, by his father's understanding, which is to govern him till he hath it of his own.

You should be laughing with tears streaming down your face at this point, after that penetrating glimpse into the obvious. But it's worse than that. It's much, much worse: When Locke sat writing that, he knew damned well that children born to the very slaves he was trading in—being bound, branded, and shipped across seas like cattle at the moment he wrote it—would be born as slaves. He also knew damned well that the children of the "leet-men" that *Locke himself had created* in the Carolina constitution would be born as "leet-men"—serfs, servants, indentured under the domination of their "lords"—should his "constitution" actually go into effect. In his bottomless tar of hypocrisy, though, in his tortured mental writhings that poisoned his writings, he contradicted himself *again*, just paragraphs further on:

> The freedom then of man, and liberty of acting according to his own will, is grounded on his having reason, which is able to instruct him in that law he is to govern himself by, and make him know how far he is left to the freedom of his own will.

And now we're back to "reason" being the infamous "law of nature" that makes us all "equal and independent"—except we aren't when born, until somehow, at some point, through some mystical process, we are. Apparently the "law of nature" which is "the law of God" doesn't get around to kicking in until some arbitrary age. (It seems that nobody ever bothered to tell John Locke that all of Egypt, for instance, was ruled at times by people who hadn't even reached their teens.)

If you want more of John Locke's sticky madness, it's easy to find; wade in it; immerse yourself in it; ride round and round and round on it. There's only so much of it that can be injected here, though, without it infecting like a fever, but the above is plenty to demonstrate the absurdity of the "independent" part of his "equal and independent" lunacy, if only in relation to the utterly *dependent* state of a newborn child. But it goes much, much farther than that.

No *parent* of any human being ever has ever been otherwise than utterly *dependent* on *another* human being in order to become a *parent* at all.

No human being can remain insularly within only the confines of the *birth family*, or there will be no opportunity to find *viable mates*, so the very nature of being *human* compels *interdependence* among human beings in order to continue the race. Every human being also is utterly *dependent* upon the existence of animals or plants or both even to stay alive—whether a parent or not.

All human procreation is utterly dependent on human *interdependence*.

All business and commerce is utterly dependent on human *interdependence*.

All monetary systems are utterly dependent on human *interdependence*.

All science is utterly dependent on human *interdependence*.

All art is utterly dependent on human *interdependence*.

All literature is utterly dependent on human *interdependence*.

All entertainment is utterly dependent on human *interdependence*.

All politics is utterly dependent on human *interdependence*.

All society and culture is utterly dependent on human *interdependence*.

"Independent"? Codswollop! John Donne had it right, if only the world had listened to him instead of to a madman like Locke:

No man is an island,
Entire of itself,
Every man is a piece of the continent,
A part of the main.
If a clod be washed away by the sea,
Europe is the less.
As well as if a promontory were.
As well as if a manor of thy friend's
Or of thine own were:
Any man's death diminishes me,
Because I am involved in mankind,
And therefore never send to know for whom the bell tolls;
It tolls for thee.

Equality Negates independence; Independence Negates equality

Even a moment outside the narcotic influence of the Grand Priests of Academia—who peddle this poisonous Lockean swill like drug pushers, as though it were the elixir of life—will tell any rational thinking person that it is patently impossible to be both "equal" and "independent," because it would be *impossible* even to determine "equality" without *interaction*, which very fact of interaction would produce immediate *interdependence*, which *interdependence* would immediately introduce some factor of *inequality*, because there cannot possibly be any *interaction* in this universe absent a plus and a minus.

Period.

Not one generation of a single erg of energy, not one interchange of any description, *ever* has occurred in this universe without a *positive* and a *negative* polarity held apart by some kind of base. All of life and motion—*all* of it, whether you believe it is the product of a soul, or of God, or of some magical mixture of nothing but chemicals and synergy—depends *entirely* on the ultimate *inequality*: a plus and a minus.

Period.

So "equality" and "independence" are *mutually exclusive*.

Period.

That's just how droolingly deranged John Locke's "philosophy"

CREATED EQUAL: THE GREATEST LIE

is, yet every university and college in the world is pumping this poison into the minds of students, right now, as you read this.

It's as though Locke rhetorically held two opposing poles of a cosmic electric dynamo so they were almost touching, and the blinding arc threw the world into a state of shock from which it never has recovered. He's the real Father of the Big Bang. The really Big Bang. We're in the middle of it still.

The worst of it is that Locke had many celebrated disciples, only one amongst them being Thomas Jefferson. At least Jefferson and his mates, by the force of their good intentions and creativity, managed to convert such drooling stupidity into something that was better than any form of government that had gone before—even with the deadly fallacy of "all men are created equal." Other Locke disciples have nearly destroyed mankind, and they all should be enshrined forever in the Hall of Infamy. One of them was Charles Darwin.

And with him, the "equality" dogma nearly gets clubbed to death.

6. Survival of the Equalist
Evolution and "Equality": The Case for Unnatural Selection

John Locke's primary justification—if it can be called such—for his mad manifesto of "equality" amongst men was his own whim, peculiar to him at the time, that man is merely a category of *animal.*

This work has already quoted one of Locke's sly implications that man is nothing but a certain brand of beast. He was very cagey and covert about it—pretending, as he was, to be a Christian—but here, by example, is another of his oily allusions to it, in the contexts of human conjugal relationships, from *Second Treatise on Government* (bold emphasis added):

> Herein I think lies the chief, if not the only reason, "why the male and female in mankind are tied to a longer conjunction" than **other creatures** ... . But though these are ties upon mankind, which make the conjugal bonds more firm and lasting in man, than the **other species of animals** ...

Try, first, to get past the arrogance of this jackass pretending that he has some insight into "conjugal bonds": That wicked whim above follows his circular and manifestly madder decree, in the same work, that "creatures of the same species" in nature are "equal one amongst another." Are you laughing yet? If not, you're probably a professor in the "social sciences," in which case you might have heaved the book across the room. Tough.

If you *are* laughing—and you should be if you've ever once stepped out into daylight—pause for one sobering reminder: This self-validating Lockean lunacy is actually taught in universities, even revered, as brilliant "philosophy." *All* of the "social sciences" being taught today are built entirely on this exact demented "foundation"—which doesn't exist.

The prophetic George Orwell exhibited rare insight in his 1945 political satire *Animal Farm,* wherein the pigs running the farm government issue a decree: "All animals are equal, but some animals are more equal than others." Despite all the critical praise and the popularity that Orwell managed to achieve, it seems that the "leaders" of academia and polity are too pigheaded in their own thinking to learn the lesson.

Like them, John Locke should have spent more time in the wild and less in dim parlors thinking dim thoughts. For him to make such a barking-mad assertion, it's difficult to imagine that he ever stuck his sickly, pasty face outside at all. Animal survival is one long struggle against the elements and against so-called "equals" for food and mates and territory.

And the less fit perish.

Exonerating Aristotle

Some "authorities" try to attribute the "man as merely animal" dogma to Aristotle, claiming that Aristotle referred to mankind as "a social animal," or "a political animal," depending on which translation you choose—but both translations are biased and wrong, and they very likely were done by people who had read Locke.

This work will not enter the no-exit labyrinth of guesses, speculation, claims, and counterclaims concerning the provenance and verity of the body of writings that today purport to be the works of Aristotle, but in almost all consensus, the Greek word that Aristotle used, where modern "translations" claim he referred to man as an "animal," was ζῷον. Every authoritative Greek lexicon supplies a *primary* definition of that Greek word as "living being" or "living thing"—*not* "animal" or "beast," which are *secondary* definitions:

Living thing. —*Woodhouse's English-Greek Dictionary*

A living being, animal. —**H. G. Liddell, R. Scott,** *A Greek-English Lexicon*

1. a living being 2. an animal, brute, beast. — *Thayer's Greek Lexicon*

A *living* creature (literally, "being *alive*"). ... ("*living* creature") is *mis*translated "beast"; better, "living being" or "living creature." — *The HELPS Lexicon*

The very duality and ambiguity of that Greek word has made it possible for biased materialist "scholars" and psychotic psychiatrists (but I repeat myself) to reverse-engineer Aristotle, using him in a reprehensibly dishonest "appeal to authority" to assert that man is nothing more than another class of animal, brute, beast.

No matter how many permanent Gordian knots (with a Mobius twist) such modern scholastic "experts" and "authorities" on philosophy tie themselves into asserting that Aristotle classified man as an "animal," in all their hundreds of thousands of agonized words analyzing Aristotle not one of them ever has been able to evade or explain away the fact that Aristotle unequivocally put mankind into a completely *separate* classification from any beast. He defined that separate classification in terms of intellect—thought, mind, *nous,* quality of the soul—with some "portion" of that intellect being both immortal and non-material, able to exist separately from the physical body, and even from matter itself. Here are three different translations of relevant statements from Aristotle's "On the Soul *(De Anima)*", III-5—which materialists try with all their might to wish away:

There is an intellect ... which is so by producing all things ... . And this intellect is distinct [from matter], unaffected, and unmixed ... . It is not the case that it sometimes thinks and at other times not. In separation it is just what it is, and this alone is immortal and eternal.
    Aristotle, De Anima Books II and III (with passages from Book I)
    Translated with Introduction and Notes by D. W. Hamlyn
    Clarendon Press, Oxford University Press

One sort of mind exists by ... making all things ... . And this mind is separable (chéristos) [from matter], unaffected, and unmixed ... . It is not the case that it sometimes thinks and sometimes does not think. Having been separated (chéristheis) this is alone what it is, and this alone is immortal and eternal.
    The Oxford Handbook of Aristotle
    edited by Christopher Shields
    Oxford University Press

One sort of mind exists ... by producing all things ... . And this mind is separate [from matter] and unaffected and unmixed ... . It is not the case that

sometimes it thinks and sometimes it does not. And having been separated, this alone is just as it is, and this alone is deathless and everlasting.
Stanford Encyclopedia of Philosophy
"The Active Mind of De Anima iii 5"
Supplement to "Aristotle's Psychology"

So, no: Aristotle is found NOT GUILTY of having relegated human beings to merely another category of animal among the beasts.

It was John Locke who perverted Aristotle's view of man as a rational and social living being, reducing man to a beast of the field. It was John Locke who set out to eradicate, in so-called philosophy, all decent and honest recognition of the eternal spiritual nature, intellect, and ethics of mankind that sets us apart from beasts.

Even the most materialistic materialist has an abiding faith—stronger even than some "religious" faiths—in a no-see-um mystery called "synergy" that somehow, some way, through some mystical process that any alchemist would marvel at, can transmute collections of sightless, senseless sparks, quarks, atoms, photons, neutrons, protons, and morons into some magical chemical combination that suddenly can see, smell, taste, feel, hear, and think.

STRANGE INTERLUDE: This brings me to something I'm going to call *Materialists' Conundrum No. 1*. Materialists and "skeptics" (also called—of themselves, by themselves, for themselves—"scientists") are all about "repeatability" and "reproducibility." They will sort of switch these two terms around, like a shell game, as convenient, but their aloof attitude is that nothing has any "scientific" validity whatsoever if it cannot be demonstrated repeatedly "under the same conditions, and in a short period of time." Natch. They use this "test" all the time to scoff at and ridicule almost anything having to do with spiritual or "paranormal" abilities. Their overarching insistence is that all such "abilities" and thought processes and senses are purely and only the result of physical, material interactions of inanimate matter, energy, and chemistry that somehow magically come together and coexist to form *life*—with sentience, growth, mobility, reproductive ability, and perception. This is their theory. Not a single one of these "scientists" *ever* has demonstrated it, though.

So *Materialists' Conundrum No. 1* is simply this: Take any combination whatsoever of *inanimate* energy, matter, and chemicals, and demonstrate conclusively that it is seeing, tasting, smelling, hearing, feeling, and thinking independently, without human input, and then have it independently move or grow, and reproduce itself. Repeatedly. Hurry up. You've been at this materialist game for centuries now, and it's about time you create life with it. So far, you're a miserable failure. You're no better than the alchemists, so get off your asses and *prove* it, or shut up about it. You may talk among yourselves.

While I'm here, though, I'm going to propose *Materialists' Conundrum No. 2:* You, dear materialist "scientist," and everything you possibly can do any experiment of any description with, are in motion at all times. If you are doing an experiment on the face of Earth, you, and the room you are in, and every other thing around you, and all the elements of your experiment, are moving at a rate close to 1,000 mile per hour, just with the rotation of Earth—never mind its revolution around the sun, or the motion of the solar system in relation to the galaxy, or the motion of the galaxy relative to other galaxies, or ... . Well, you get the idea. Therefore: how is it *ever* possible for you to have "repeatability" or "reproducibility" in any experiment, given that it can never possibly be done in the location where it first occurred? You may talk among yourselves.

Locke's entire, if incomprehensible, argument was that all human beings were "equal and independent" by virtue of being a "creature" equivalent to any other animal on earth—except for having been given "dominion and sovereignty" over the "other" animals by the "lord and master" (whoever He/She/It was).

So who is this "lord and master"? Locke styled himself as a Christian in upbringing and faith—even though he was a fraud and an atheist. Are we back on the endless "Maker–Creator–Nature's God" merry-go-round? Has following Locke led us, once again, in a large circle, back to Genesis, back to Eden, back to Yahweh? If so, Locke's copy of the Bible must have been missing the first page, because it says there plainly, in Genesis 1:27: "And God created man in His own image." It would be an unutterable sacrilege for a *Christian* to characterize the Judeo-Christian God as an *animal*, a *beast*. So *where* does Locke's *uberequal*-man-the-animal come from? In *whose image* is man made *uberequal* as an *animal*?

Of course, we really have gone right around in a Lockean circle again, because of course the mad fantasy of man-as-an-animal is made in John Locke's image, and no one else's.

John Locke is his own "God" or "Maker" who he claimed created mankind "equal and independent"—as animals.

Barking on the *Beagle*

In January 1831, the same year that Charles Darwin left for his famous voyage on the *Beagle,* he sat through three days of written final exams at Cambridge that consisted in no small part of questions addressed to Darwin's understanding of John Locke's *An Essay Concerning Human Understanding*—an influential, if painfully confused, piece of parlor philosophy in which Locke interchangeably uses the words "mind" and "soul" until they meld into one amorphous, unnamed, and uncertain "thing" that is little more than some sort of mysterious *material* medium onto which sense impressions are recorded. In fact, it is here that Locke slaps across the face the idea that man has a soul at all, and in which he makes his most bold—if wormy—suggestion that man is nothing more than a collection of whizzing matter, proving, again, that he was a materialist and an atheist:

> They who make the soul a thinking thing, at this rate, will not make it a much more noble being than those do whom they condemn, for allowing it to be nothing but the subtilist [sic] parts of matter. ...

In *An Essay Concerning Human Understanding,* Locke also stated, in many covert ways, his concepts that appear in *Second Treatise on Government* about man being merely another category of animal— but in *An Essay Concerning Human Understanding* he pounded it home (bold emphasis added):

> This faculty of laying up and retaining the ideas that are brought into the mind, **several other animals** seem to have to a great degree, as well as man. ...
>
> He that shall place the identity of man in anything else, but, **like that of other animals,** in one fitly organized body ...
>
> And whatever is talked of other definitions, ingenious observation puts it past doubt, that the idea in our minds, of which the sound "**man**" in our mouths is the sign, **is nothing else but of an animal of such a certain form**. ...
>
> For it is certain, that, in reality, the relation is the same betwixt the begetter and the begotten, in the several races of **other animals as well as men** ...
>
> I doubt not but the meaning of the term "**man**" would be as well understood, and the idea it stands for be at least as clearly made known, as when it **is defined to be a rational animal** ... .

Given Locke's status as a pin-up boy in philosophy departments, it's also very likely that Darwin had studied Locke's *Second Treatise on Government,* where Locke had created man-the-*uberequal*-animal. It's probably impossible to confirm exactly how much influence Locke's musings—making man equal to any other animal—had on Darwin as he carefully recorded observations of animals that led to his *Origin of the Species,* chapter four of which is: "Natural Selection; or the Survival of the Fittest." With some small clues, though, it seems that Darwin was almost jealously in competition with Locke on some level, which bespeaks a considerable familiarity with Locke's works. There is a well-known quote from Darwin that mentions Locke. It was written in a notebook that Darwin never intended to have published: Notebook M (1838), 84. It said in pertinent part:

> Origin of man now proved. —Metaphysics must flourish. —He who understands baboon would do more towards metaphysics than Locke.

It sounds almost like a stab at Locke, but according to commentary at the Darwin Online website, it in fact reflects Darwin's excitement at feeling he could somehow outdo Locke:

> Emotion in animals and man. Darwin has been to the zoo. He has been there with his eyes open for animal expressions of emotion, linking man with the rest of creation in yet one more way. And he has found enough to make him exult, for it is he who will understand the baboon and outstrip the great empirical philosopher John Locke.

Ignoring, out of kindness, the amusingly unfortunate use of the phrase "the rest of **creation**" (oh, dear, there's that word again) I would have to say that Darwin certainly got the essence of baboon down in all ways; his thinking reflects it. It is a remarkable phenomenon that professors and so-called "advanced" students can read Darwin at all, much less lend him any credence, given that he was so fire-hydrant stupid as to actually write, in *The Descent of Man, Volume I:*

> There is no fundamental difference between man and the higher mammals in their mental faculties.

But then, professors and so-called "advanced" students read Locke and lend him credence, so they should be acknowledged at least for consistency in baboonery. Fortunately for the rest of us, none of the "higher mammals" ever has been caught reading Darwin at all, or Locke, for that matter, so none of them has ever learned of their amazing man-equal faculties. Shhhhh. Don't tell them.

For those of us who can read, Darwin's statement, meanwhile, is a chillingly familiar and chattering echo of John Locke.

Survival of the Fittest, or of the Equalist?

It's inconceivable that Locke's philosophical fiat proclaiming man's animalhood could have played no part in Darwin's screed. It's wonderfully ironic, though, that Locke's man-the-equal-animal theory dons the divine robes of creationism in the *Declaration of Independence,* then just 55 years later sits perched on Darwin's shoulder across the seven seas, like a pirate's parrot (perhaps a "rational parrot"?), to turn up as an inseparable component of the theory of evolution.

That inconvenient fact creates what I dub the *Materialists'*

Conundrum No. 3. I hereby hand it over to all good flag-waving, card-carrying materialists to resolve, and thereby wash my hands of it like a modern-day Pilate:

> *Materialists' Conundrum No. 3:* If man is an animal, and if all men are equal—whether created equal, evolved to alleged equality, or cosmically blown into a state of equality—and if man is equal in "mental faculties" to "the higher mammals," is evolution over?

You may talk among yourselves ...

7. Mysticism, Madness, Morals, and the Mind
Cosmic Unequalizers

Death awaits us all. Death has been called "the great equalizer." There is nothing quite so "equal" as a row of anonymous body bags. Death, though, and what might come after it, has everything to do with what *life* actually is. That question always has been the shared domain of religion and of mysticism. Theirs has been the kingdom of the human spirit, or soul as some call it—the intangible quality apart from physical existence that Aristotle took such pains to describe in his work, "On the Soul." The Greeks had a marvelous word for it, "psykhe," which became "psyche" in the Latin version and in English. In Greek it meant, literally, and beautifully, "breath." Here is a relevant excerpt from the description of its etymology, from The Online Etymology Dictionary:

> "animating spirit," from Latin *psyche,* from Greek *psykhe* "the soul, mind, spirit; breath; life, one's life, the invisible animating principle or entity which occupies and directs the physical body; understanding" ... Also in ancient Greek, "departed soul, spirit, ghost,"

As aesthetically simple and insightful as that definition is, it nonetheless disguises a possible deadly trap, a punji pit into which the unwary could fall—and many have. John Locke found that pit and filled it with tar to make it escape-proof, then covered it over with flowery, flimsy linguistic frippery to lure as many as possible to fall into it, never to emerge. The trap—and it truly is inescapable, like a pitcher plant—is rigged up by conflating the *spirit* (soul, elan vital) with the *mind*.

The *spirit* is capable of thought and perception, but it is **not** the storage repository of memory called the *mind*.

They are separate and severable. Mankind has had this instinctive and ineradicable awareness since at least as far back as the Vedic Hymns, and no one truly knows just how far back those go. Aristotle knew this over 2,000 years ago, and described the spiritual nature of man eloquently, within the confines of inadequate language, as intangible *intellect*, which some "experts" have translated as being "a *sort of* mind." Yet even those foggy translations set this quality of *spirit* (or "soul") apart from the more pedestrian concepts of "mind" and memory. And the spirit is an intangible *quality*, *not* a measureable *quantity*—which fact makes jolly jest of materialists insisting that it can't possibly exist if they can't measure it with physical meters.

As already quoted in the previous chapter, Aristotle stated that this quality—this nonmaterial and infinite potential for thought and perception and comprehension—and this alone, is "immortal and eternal," and can exist *separately,* in its entirety, from the composite known as man. In that awareness, Aristotle served and acknowledged perhaps the greatest awareness of all mankind, an awareness that has imbued and lived vibrantly within every religion ever known—and even lives within the basest, most atheistic materialism in the guise of "synergy."

John Locke, though, promiscuously, indiscriminately, recklessly throws around the terms "spirit," "soul," "mind," "brain," "animal spirit," "substance," "body," "memory," "man," "person," and "consciousness" with such wildly interchangeable abandon that it would be easier to remove the sugar from a baked and iced cake than to pull apart the gooey, sticky, lumpy mess that Locke served up, mainly in a manuscript called—and here irony simply passes out cold: *An Essay Concerning Human Understanding.*

It should forever more be known as *An Essay Concerning Human Tar.*

Now, I readily acknowledge that you have every right, at this moment, to assume that I am simply some rube, some mentally challenged dolt, some pitiable pilgrim wandering the woods of philosophy without benefit of sufficient indoctrination into the heady elitism of "higher education," and as a result, I—bless my heart—am therefore hopelessly lost, unable to grasp these elevated concepts of "understanding" that John Locke blessed the world with.

All right. On that basis, let us, together, sit in on some of the most highly educated, "peer reviewed," papered-and-parchmented "experts" in the world—all of them with the *de rigueur* "PhD" appended to their names—who are, without argument, the Highest High Priests of Lockeanism that can be found, and allow *them* to give us some insights into Locke's scripture on "Human Understanding." I'll just let them have the floor to explain to us how lucid and brilliant Locke's masterpiece on the human mind and human understanding is.

We'll turn first to a source that may be The Ultimate Authority of Authorities on Locke, because it carries on its label the august imprimatur of The Stanford Encyclopedia of Philosophy— and Stanford University has been called "one of the world's most prestigious universities" by no less an authority on authorities than the United Kingdom's *The Guardian*. If those aren't *bona fides* enough for you, Stanford has anointed itself "one of the world's leading research universities." Who is to argue?

Stanford's selected expert on Locke appears to be one William Uzgalis, who, according to his faculty page at Oregon State University, holds a "PhD in Philosophy from Stanford University." His article at the online Stanford Encyclopedia of Philosophy is titled, appropriately, "John Locke," with a supplement he authored titled "Some Issues in Locke's Philosophy of Mind." Together, the articles contain a considerable discourse on Locke's *An Essay Concerning Human Understanding*. Let us then look at a few quotes of note to enhance our understanding of human understanding—and if you think, at any moment, that I am willfully making any of this sound other than it is by selectively taking it "out of context," I invite, nay, I *urge* you to visit the source articles, which are easily found online as identified above. Let the illumination begin, and we are assured right at the outset how brilliant Locke and his "monumental" essay are:

> Locke is often classified as the first of the great English empiricists ... .
> This reputation rests on Locke's greatest work, the monumental *An Essay Concerning Human Understanding*. ...
>
> Locke ... argues that we have no innate knowledge. (In this he resembles Berkeley and Hume, and differs from Descartes and Leibniz.) ...

Well, as long as Locke is in agreement with some, but in disagreement with others, we can be certain that we are safely in the bosom of the aristocracy of academia. We proceed ...

> Locke's first point is that if propositions were innate they should be immediately perceived—by infants and idiots (and indeed everyone else)—but there is no evidence that they are. ...

We, dear reader, being neither infants nor idiots (we hope), should have a head start in this perception-of-propositions game, but we will have to just close our eyes and be led along, hoping that this isn't just an unseemly proposition (wink, wink) ...

> Locke says little about who holds the doctrine of innate principles that he is attacking. For this reason he has sometimes been accused of attacking straw men. John Yolton has persuasively argued (Yolton, 1956) ...

Whenever I leave a quoted thought incomplete, as just above, I beseech to look at it not as though you have been deprived, but as though you have been spared. You can hunt up Yolton if you would like to find out what he argued, but suffice it here to say that he argued. And now, we can only hold hope that the straw men being mentioned have some brains (wink, wink) ...

> The charge that Locke's account of innate principles is made of straw, is not a just criticism. ...
>
> Complex ideas are of two kinds, ideas of substances and ideas of modes. ...
>
> Beings that count as substances include God, angels, humans, animals, plants and a variety of constructed things. ...

Perhaps it will come as a great sigh of relief to any materialists following along with us on this Yellow Brick Road to learn from Locke-once-removed that God is a *substance*. I will merely add, humbly, if I may, that so are lions and tigers and bears, oh my! And perhaps even flying monkeys, and the Wicked Witch of the West ...

> He [Locke] is telling us that we may never be able to know whether dualist or materialist theories of mind are true. If we can't know which position is true, that would seem to be the end of it. ...

Hm. That would seem to me to be the poppy field, and we all may as well just lie down and go into a coma. Where is Glinda the Good Witch and her wonderful wand when you need her? (Not that we don't already have a snow job in progress.) No Glinda in sight—but here comes Nicolas Jolley! Maybe he can save us ...

> Nicholas Jolley argues that a variety of different passages ... suggest that Locke is trying to show that a weak form of materialism is a plausible candidate in the Philosophy of Mind. ...

Or maybe not ...

> Locke is telling us that both possibilities, thinking matter and immaterial thinking substance, are beyond our comprehension ...

Does this mean we are infants or idiots, or perhaps just that we are hopelessly stupid? Wait: Did he just say "thinking matter"? I think (whether I'm matter or otherwise) that there may be another Materialists' Conundrum bubbling up out of the tar ...

> The thinking matter hypothesis disturbed a number of Locke's early critics (and some later ones). ...

He did say "thinking matter"! He did! Oh, there definitely is another Materialists' Conundrum taking shape in the tar, like a giant tar baby rising up out of it (not to mix fairy tales).

> What is it that God adds (or in Locke's technical language) superadds to matter fitly disposed to make it perceive and think? ...

There's Glinda the Good Witch now! Finally! No, wait: That's not Glinda; it's God. Different robes. I apologize to any materialists/atheists following along with us. I should have seen this coming and warned you. This truly is a *deus ex machina*—a god from a machine that has popped up like a Jack-in-the-Box as an answer to everything. But at least we are having human understanding explained to us, according to Locke, by some of the smartest people in the world ...

It would appear from this account that, in respect to material bodies, superadded properties are those God adds to matter to create certain kinds of things beyond the essence of matter, that yet leaves the essence of matter unaffected. Locke's God is a clockmaker ...

This model of superaddition makes one wonder what exactly it is that God is adding to the matter fitly disposed. It seems that there are no very good answers. ...

"It seems that there are no very good answers"? It would certainly be appreciated if you at Stanford—and at all the other colleges and universities selling this snake oil—would put that in big bold red letters right on the front of your sales brochures and web sites that you use gyp people out of large sums of money.

But reader, while we're here: Did you notice a certain little phrase go slipping by above? Here it is again: "Superadded properties are those God adds to matter to create certain kinds of things beyond the essence of matter." Do you know what the materialists/scientists/skeptics/atheists call that? You're way out ahead of me now, aren't you? Yes, they call it "synergy."

Now: How long do we have to stand here pounding on the door to this Emerald City gate to get somebody to open it and let us inside the Inner Sanctum Sanctorum of higher knowledge so we can have a human understanding of human understanding? Hang on: I think I hear someone coming ...

Margaret Wilson pointed out that Locke sees limits to Boylean mechanism in Locke's discussion of thinking matter. (Wilson, 1999, p. 199) The problem is just that the banging together of pieces of matter cannot explain perception and thought. ...

Oh, well then; that's a horse of a different color!

Let me pause for a moment to assure you emphatically that I am not intentionally making comedy here by my selection of quotes to comment on. These are deadly serious discussions by learned professors about things taught very soberly in institutions of higher learning that cost tens of thousands of dollars to attend (even though the institutions are subsidized by tax dollars), so no laughing! The experts go on (and they do go on):

> Given that God is using some other way to connect motions and colors, it does not follow that the connections are arbitrary, though they seem so to us. So, a divine understanding of nature might still be possible. ...

Are we about to be admitted to meet the Great Wizard? Finally! Finally!

> Many of Locke's critics were suspicious that Locke had materialist tendencies. ... Samuel Clarke ... engaged in a debate by correspondence or rather public pamphlet with Anthony Collins over this issue ... For accounts of this debate see Yolton (1983) and Martin and Baresi (2000) ... Edwin McCann has argued that Locke's general account of identity is intended to supply a corpuscularian alternative to the Aristotelian account of identity ... . Udo Thiel ... provides a massive study of the possible sources and influences on Locke's account of personal identity ...

Nope. Sorry. Just a room full of "experts" arguing—or having a "disputation," as Locke liked to call it. Let's move on in the maze ...

> Locke's principle allows God, a soul and a body all to be in one place at the same time for each of them belongs to one of the three different kinds of substances ...

Hm. Sounds very much like it could be a wizard to me. Or possibly a Good Witch. Or possibly a Fairy Godmother. Or maybe Buddha. No, wait! Wait! Could this be that we're back to the Trinity—three-in-one at the same time? But what do I know? Let the High Priests of Human Understanding preach and teach ...

> Some commentators would like to take "kind" to mean the nominal essences of Book III of the Essay ... . But were that the case a horse and an elephant, which have different nominal essences, could be in the same place at the same time! ...
>
> If living things and masses ... are both bodies, then we have two things of the same kind (bodies) in the same place at the same time! For a discussion of the various ways that have been proposed to solve this problem see Stewart (2013) and Gordon-Roth (2015) ...
>
> Absolute identity theorists hold that individuative criteria for different kinds are the unity conditions for that kind ... . They hold that relative identity is, in fact, an incoherent doctrine. ...

I pray, fervently, that your own understanding of John Locke's "monumental" explanation of human understanding is now growing, joyously, by leaps and bounds—to coin a phrase—under the guidance of these erudite and educated shepherds. Oh, here's another one now:

> Peter Geach first suggested that Locke's account of identity should be understood in terms of relative identity. ...
>   Can one say that this individual horse (x) is the same horse as that (y) but not the same mass of matter, even though both x and y are horses and masses of matter?

There are our horses of different color, now gone all the way around the circle and back again! Except it seems that they are carousel horses. And now we can finally understand Locke's Human Understanding: It's a merry-go-round to nowhere sinking into the tar. Listen a moment more to the hissing, squeaky calliope music ...

> The same issue applies to man and mass of matter, and soul and person. The most recent defender of the relative identity position is Stewart (2013). ... Locke is saying that the substance that thinks in us could be any one of the eight combinations of possibilities ... Why Locke rejects the claim that having the same soul is a necessary condition for personal identity is not as clear. ...

Not clear? Not clear! Why, it's as clear as tar! Let's just quietly close the door and allow these experts to slip burbling and gurgling into their well-earned fate, shall we? Are you all clear on this now? Any questions? Well, we have barely dipped a toe into the Lockean tar pit of "human understanding," and not very far out in that pit, swirling with a menacing burble and gurgle, is the *real* sucking vortex of the pit, the ultimate black hole for the soul and the mind, the maddest madness yet encountered:

John Locke's "White Paper"
John Locke took some perfectly good white paper, and by writing on it made it entirely worthless. (My deepest apologies to Ludwig von Mises, who allegedly said [often attributed to Mark Twain]: "Government is the only institution that can take a valuable commodity like paper, and make it worthless by applying ink.")

Perhaps the loopiest lunacy of Lockean literature is a concept that he simply stole from other theorists who had gone before him, which he then twisted and perverted and mashed down into his *An*

Essay Concerning Human Understanding tar. Below are two slightly different versions of this Lockean lunacy—the very fact of the subtle differences, indicated with bold, giving an almost laughable indication of the texture of all this tar. Here first is the passage quoted from the Liberty Fund's version of Locke's *An Essay Concerning Human Understanding*, citation following:

> Let us then suppose the mind to be, as we say, white paper, void of all characters, without any ideas; how comes it to be furnished? Whence comes it by that vast store which the busy and boundless fancy of man has painted on it, with an almost endless variety? Whence has it all the materials of reason and knowledge? To this I answer, in one word, from experience; **in all that our knowledge is founded**, and from that it ultimately derives itself.
> John Locke, *The Works of John Locke in Nine Volumes*, (London: Rivington, 1824 12th ed.). Vol. 1. February 18, 2017. http://oll. libertyfund.org/titles/761

Now here is another version, prepared by Pennsylvania State University, citation following:

> Let us then suppose the mind to be, as we say, white paper, void of all characters, without any ideas:—How comes it to be furnished? Whence comes it by that vast store which the busy and boundless fancy of man has painted on it with an almost endless variety? Whence has it all the materials of reason and knowledge? To this I answer, in one word, from experience. **In that all our knowledge is founded**; and from that it ultimately derives itself.
> *An Essay Concerning Human Understanding* by John Locke (First published 1690), the Pennsylvania State University, Electronic Classics Series, Jim Manis, Faculty Editor, Hazleton, PA 18201-1291 is a Portable Document File produced as part of an ongoing student publication project to bring classical works of literature, in English, to free and easy access of those wishing to make use of them.

You may think that I'm nitpicking to make bold those two slightly different phrases, and I certainly am not attempting to make them more than they are; I isolate them only to alert you to the subtle and easily missed differences that exist in many different "versions" of Locke's works. Some of the versions actually have been *rewritten* with the claimed purpose of making them "easier to understand"—just as though it's possible to understand them at all. In this relatively minor highlighted difference, it yet does change the meaning of the sentence. That, though, is hardly worth bothering with in the roiling frothy insanity contained in Locke's "white paper" dogma.

It's hard to know exactly where to start because this "white paper" waste of paper is nothing at all but more circular and entirely self-validating gibberish. The "experts" like to refer to this "white paper" concept with the hoity-toity Latin-derived term *tabula rasa,* which, loosely translated, means "blank slate," or "clean slate," such as an ancient wax writing tablet on which nothing has been inscribed or that has been wiped smooth. There is an infinite supply of irony in looking at Locke because he can hardly write an arbitrary decree without contradicting one of his other arbitrary decrees, so I'll just pick this—arbitrarily—as an entrance point: Locke is the single worst excuse for an "empiricist" that ever has existed.

Let's return for just a moment to the fanboy fawning of Stanford's product, Dr. Uzgalis, quoted above: "Locke is often classified as the first of the great English empiricists." Then God save England, and God save empiricism, and God save us all.

Empiricism is defined in philosophy as "the doctrine that all knowledge is derived from sense experience," and this is the biggest merry-go-round to nowhere ever erected, because apparently neither John Locke nor any "empiricist" since has ever once opened their eyes and *looked* at anything. If any of them had, they *would have* immediately tossed John Locke onto a goat cart and trundled him off to Bedlam the instant he bleated that we are all "equal and independent." And that insane claim—however insane it may be and certainly is, all by itself—is instantly negated the moment you buy into this *new insanity* that all we ever are when born is a *blank slate* with *no innate knowledge.*

And here, risen up from the tar as a black and dripping behemoth, comes Materialists' Conundrum No. 4, presented as four questions:

How *in the hell,* then, do you propose to claim that we all are *independent?*

Who *the hell* is supposed to "write" something onto this "blank slate," if we all are both "independent" and "equal"?

How *in the hell* are we supposed to know how to have *any sense perceptions at all* if we have *no innate knowledge?*

How *in the hell* does anyone get stupid enough to buy into such garbage? (Wait, actually I know the answer to that one: public school, which is now run by psychologists and psychiatrists, the biggest psycho lunatics of all.)

No child—or kitten, for that matter—has to be taught how to breathe.

No newborn baby—or calf, for that matter—has to be taught to lock onto a teat.

No baby has to be taught to see. That is innate knowledge.

No baby has to be taught to hear. That is innate knowledge.

No baby has to be taught to feel. That is innate knowledge.

No baby has to be taught to taste. That is innate knowledge.

No baby has to be taught to smell. That is innate knowledge.

No baby has to be taught the sensation of falling. That is innate knowledge.

No baby has to be taught the sensation of temperature. That is innate knowledge.

No baby has to be taught to eliminate waste from the body. That is innate knowledge.

No baby has to be taught to move his limbs. That is innate knowledge.

This list could go on long enough to form its own book, with nothing else, and anybody could formulate such a list, if only they will compile it from their own *observation* of actual *life*, not from the voices in their heads or dusty, moldy books.

There are a thousand thousand things in real life that absolutely decimate, shred, explode Locke's nutty "white paper" theory of "human understanding," which is no "understanding" whatsoever. It is lunacy.

Just one of those things is the creation of science fiction and fantasy. There's not a single chance in hell that imaginative science fiction and fantasy ever derived from any sensory experience—at least not in one human lifetime. The postulation of past lifetimes of the spirit, when interstellar space opera may have been a reality, or when and where dragons or elves walked and lived, certainly provides a complete explanation for all of it, if memory of experience is its source—but don't try to mention that to an "empiricist." (Also, please don't tell them that John Locke himself said this, found in *The Life and Letters of John Locke* by Lord King: "The magicians of Egypt turned their rods into serpents as well as Moses." Locke, naturally, never even attempted an explanation.)

Another thing that shatters the "blank slate" lunacy is the entire field of the visual arts. Duchamp sure as hell never saw a nude descending a staircase that looked anything at all like his famous painting of one. He created a new "reality," an alternate "reality," that was not—could not possibly be—anything that came to him from the external world in sense perception. The very idea is absurd. The same could be said of every song or musical composition ever written: It never, ever existed to be experienced by the artist, or by anyone, before the artist *conceived and created it*, and brought it into a physical existence through the vibrations that create sound.

Another *massive* body of data that makes laughingstock of the materialists' *tabula rasa* theory is everything to do with the paranormal—which is a terrible misnomer, because so much of what is classified as "paranormal" by materialistic "empiricists" really is merely normal for a huge swath of the population of man, and always has been. There is hardly a person walking who has not "known," for example, of a phone about to ring, and of who will be calling, when absolutely no "standard" sensory perception could predict it. The literature of history is awash, flooded, with stories of extrasensory perception and extra-human abilities, and to this very moment there is no "scientific explanation" that explains any of these magnificent phenomena in a way that even a moron would accept (except, perhaps, one with a PhD). Yet there are, quite literally, millions of words recording human *experience*—well, there's that damned word come back to haunt the "empiricists"—in just such phenomena, subjective and objective. The "empiricists" simply *refuse to accept* any of it. Why? Because it would destroy their religious Cult of Empiricist Materialism.

Another of those things that destroys the Lockean lunacy is the phenomenon of the child prodigy. There is a *massive* list of them available—and those are just the ones that have earned some sort of notoriety or fame. It wouldn't come as any surprise if you've been aware of some particularly gifted or talented person just in your own life that may never have made it onto any "authority's" list, but who nonetheless exhibited talents, skills, or abilities that absolutely soar beyond anything that could have been "taught"—written onto that alleged "blank slate"—by anyone within their reach. How do we know it could not possibly have been "taught"? *Because no one anywhere near them ever exhibited any such talent or skill or ability!* That's as obvious as the Grand Canyon!

But what do our vaunted, educated, degreed "empiricists" do with such blatantly obvious information? They eject it from consideration, or "explain" it away with more gibberish, or opine that some never-before-seen random combination of particles of matter and chemicals just happened somehow to bang themselves together, like billiard balls, in just the right combination to produce the Sistine Chapel ceiling or the pitch-perfect rendition of Paganini's Caprice No. 4 in C Minor by an 8-year-old.

Where do we get such gullible clods as these worshipped and adored "empiricists"? From public schools and universities, that's where. Let's not leave this to chance, though, because if you attempt to pin one of these Lockean cultists down on this Cult of Empiricist Materialism, they will wriggle away to jump on another merry-go-round to nowhere, catcalling back at you that they have escaped your inspection. For example, there is the following merry-go-round—and we won't ride it; we'll just stand here at the side and watch it for a moment go round and round and round. This, briefly, comes from another "authority": The Internet Encyclopedia of Philosophy. They have a very high opinion of themselves, to wit:

> The staff of 30 editors and approximately 300 authors hold doctorate degrees and are professors at universities around the world, most notably from English-speaking countries. ... The submission and review process of articles is the same as that with printed philosophy journals, books and reference works. The authors are specialists in the areas in which they write, and are frequently leading authorities. Submissions are peer reviewed by

specialists according to strict criteria. The peer review process is rigorous and meets high academic standards.

Thank whatever gods may be—or whoever you thank—that we, the Great Unwashed, don't have to stand in the same room with them for fear of giving offense, but we simply must, even as heathens and heretics, peek while we can at their Great Circular Carnival Ride of Peer-Reviewed Philosophical Truths of All Truths to find out what they decree about Locke's "white paper" dogma. So gird your loins. Keeping in mind all the phenomena in life and the world that shatters such materialistic hogwash, yet here it is:

> There is one misunderstanding which it is important to avoid when considering Locke's anti-nativism. The misunderstanding is, in part, suggested by Locke's claim that the mind is like a *tabula rasa* (a blank slate) prior to sense experience. This makes it sound as though the mind is nothing prior to the advent of ideas. In fact, Locke's position is much more nuanced. He makes it clear that the mind has any number of inherent capacities, predispositions, and inclinations prior to receiving any ideas from sensation. His anti-nativist point is just that none of these is triggered or exercised until the mind receives ideas from sensation. ...

Aren't we foolish hayseeds, then, for missing out on all of that nuance! And I hate to be a troublemaker; I simply loathe the idea of daring to question these berobed and Holy Holders of the Great and Unassailable Truths of All Truths—but: Twisting me hat in me hands, and scuffing me toes with downcast eyes, I must yet mention, if only in 'umble passing, that not one of the "30 editors and approximately 300 authors" holding doctorate degrees ever got around to saying where these "inherent capacities, predispositions, and inclinations" came from. Begging yer pardon, yer 'onor! No doubt just a minor oversight! Y'all were probably just too busy peer-reviewing each other to mention it. (If Darwin gave the world nothing else from his heroic hours standing by the baboon cages, at least we know the importance of peer review.) Carry on ...

> We are now in a position to understand the character of Locke's empiricism. He is committed to the view that all of our ideas, everything we can possibly think of, can be broken down into simple ideas received in experience. ...
>
> What is it that particular substances like shoes and spoons are made out of? We could suggest that they are made out of leather and metal. But

> the question could be repeated, what are leather and metal made of? We
> might respond that they are made of matter. But even here, Locke thinks
> we can ask what matter is made of. What gives rise to the properties of
> matter? Locke claims that we don't have a very clear idea here. So our idea
> of substances will always be somewhat confused ... .

"Don't have a very clear idea here"? "Somewhat confused"? Really? You think?

No, you peer-reviewed posers: Shoes are made solely (pun intended) out of *creative thought,* as are spoons, the first ones made by human beings who never had seen or heard of or experienced a shoe or a spoon before, because they *didn't exist to be experienced!*

Reader: You are a soldier to slog through this tar with me, and I'm sorry to have had to drag you along, but one important reason that your understanding of this materialistic, empiricist "understanding" of human understanding cannot responsibly be left to chance is because you may not be aware that the entire subject and profession of today's psychology and psychiatry—*all* of it—is built *entirely* on this "foundation" of Lockean tar.

And there isn't a teacher teaching at any level today in the United States that is allowed into a classroom without having first been indoctrinated in "educational psychology," all of which is built *entirely* on this bed of Lockean tar.

And there isn't a textbook published that isn't approved by a board consisting of one or more psychologists or psychiatrists, all of them thoroughly hip-deep in this dogma.

And there isn't a public school standing that is otherwise than under the "guidance" of one or a hundred of these Lockean loons.

And that's exactly why "schools" today are not engaged in education, but in Lockean, empiricist, materialist social engineering, designed, with malice aforethought, to pound the brightest and the best down into the tar of Lockean "equality" with the dullest and most debased.

And their Grand Priest of Propaganda Programming for Children is a sadistic German torturer named Wilhelm Wundt.

Wilhelm Wundt: The Grand Priest of Lockean Lunacy

Until 1879, psychology (the very word originally meaning study of the spirit, or soul) stood together with religion and mysticism as far as interest in and care of man's spiritual nature was concerned. It was Wilhelm Wundt who that year hijacked the word "psychology" and redefined it to assert that man had no *psyche* at all, but was merely a material recording device for external stimuli. Does that sound somehow vaguely familiar?

Yes, Wundt was another Locke disciple whose materialistic model of man and his mind was so precisely a carbon copy of Locke's "white paper" premise that Wundt expended pages and pages of ponderous, pompous, and prolix prose obfuscating the fact that the entire idea was a nothing more than nebulous philosophical pipe dream—one that still has nothing more to support it than does the Indian rope trick above a bed or tar. *All* of psychiatry is built on it.

I'm going to take the cheeky liberty of quoting myself. This comes from chapter 11, "The Coldest War: The Battle for Men's Souls," of my book *Watergate: The Hoax,* because it's precisely germane:

> In 1892, Wilhelm Wundt, who has been called "the father of experimental psychology," had disdainfully dismissed the idea that "the human spirit is a sensible being, separable from the body," attributing such notions to "primitive races." In 1911 he went further, stating with the kingly arrogance of self-appointed, self-anointed thought-totalitarians that the "soul can no longer exist in the face of our present-day physiological knowledge."
>
> Well. That settled that—at least to his fellow thought-totalitarians of the psycho- establishment. Psychologists and psychiatrists rushed to proclaim and parrot their new religion-masquerading-as-science: Man is nothing more than an animal, a soulless collection of meat and chemicals. With the fervor of cultish proselytizers, the psycho-establishment goose-stepped into the 20th century to the beat of the Wundtian drum, and became as soulless as the man-animals it tried to shock, drug, carve, restrain, reward, punish, and beat into rat-maze submission. (The only problem is that it never seemed to work.)

Wundt did nice little things to his captive man-animals—like set 10,000 green blocks, one after another, in front of his helpless and hapless experimental subjects, just to see how they reacted. Psychology and psychiatry, suddenly set free of even the flimsiest bonds of human decency or ethics, then enthusiastically submitted human "animals" to lobotomies, electroshock, and deadly mind- and mood-altering drugs—their "application" of the "science" of *tabula rasa*: "By god, we'll rewrite that man's mind the way we think it ought to be, or we'll damned well destroy it, or drug it into compliance or stupor!"

Lockean-Wundtian "theory" was the sole and only source of idiotic and perfectly evil "stimulus-response" theories and practice that followed, from Pavlov to Skinner, treating man as merely another animal that could be trained like a rat in a maze. If you think for a moment that all of that is now passé—which is what the psycho-establishment propagandists are always selling, along with their latest flavor-of-the-month theory—the "stimulus-response," carrot-and-stick dogma is in full-blown use right this minute in every government and school in the world.

In the late 1940s and early 1950s, the CIA and its predecessors became the primary consumers of the psycho-establishment's methods of torture-and-drug-and-hypnotize in attempts to create human automatons who would carry out criminal political operations without morals or question, but I've covered that in Watergate: The Hoax, and am not going to visit it further here.

The dirty little secret that the psycho-establishment carefully keeps from you—well, one of their dirty little secrets—is that all of their efforts, all of them, are supposedly to make a patient "normal," yet not one of them, anywhere in the world, has any standard of what "normal" is. "Normal" is whatever their paymaster or the latest drug from Big Pharma says is "normal." Anything else at all, on their whims, can be classed, then, as "abnormal" or "dysfunctional," and so they have created a big, big book—the size of which now is in competition with the Christian Bible—categorizing just about every possible human emotion, reaction, or manifestation as some kind of emotional or psychological "condition" needing their sweet, loving "treatment." They are the makers of "madness" so they can elevate themselves as the High Priests of madness. They no doubt learned it from Locke.

In the same collection of Locke's ravings we've already been dealing with in this chapter, *An Essay Concerning Human Understanding*, he had the audacity to write out this sick and twisted "anecdote":

> A friend of mine knew one perfectly cured of madness by a very harsh and offensive operation. The gentleman, who was thus recovered, with great sense of gratitude and acknowledgment, owned the cure all his life after, as the greatest obligation he could have received; but whatever gratitude and reason suggested to him, he could never bear the sight of the operator: that image brought back with it the idea of that agony which he suffered from his hands, which was too mighty and intolerable for him to endure.

Who was this "friend"? No one knows, or even bothers to question. Who was this friend-of-a-friend who was "perfectly cured of madness by a very harsh and offensive operation"? No one knows, or even bothers to question. What was the nature of this "very harsh and offensive operation" that provided a "cure" for "madness"? No one knows or even bothers to question. This lunatic claim is accepted on blind faith as though Locke were speaking through a burning bush, and your children are being force-fed this offal as though it were the very Word of God in institutions that tout themselves as being the sanctum sanctorum of science and secular sanity.

In the very same fustian folderol, Locke took his saner-than-thou insanity even further, trying to find solace for his own madness by declaring that all men have madness in them:

> I shall be pardoned for calling it by so harsh a name as madness, when ... opposition to reason deserves that name, and is really madness; and there is scarce a man so free from it, but that if he should always ... argue or do as in some cases he constantly does, would not be thought fitter for Bedlam than civil conversation. ... And if this be a weakness to which all men are so liable; if this be a taint which so universally infects mankind; the greater care should be taken to lay it open under its due name, thereby to excite the greater care in its prevention and cure.

No, it is *not* "a weakness to which all men are so liable," just as "all men" are not created equal. Locke himself manifestly had such madness, so there is little wonder that he wanted to comfort himself by claiming that we all are "equal," and therefore equally mad. That is an exquisite madness in itself.

But supposedly educated people read this baboon-chatter (apologies, if due, to Darwin), and never even notice the irony that

John Locke is the same babbling liar who mere paragraphs before had claimed that someone could be "perfectly cured of madness." Philosopher, heal thyself, then.

Locke himself certainly had enough madness to spread around to everybody in the world. And he did.

As a direct result today, right now, every minute, there is some drug pusher somewhere with a PhD stuck behind his name and a framed dusty degree on his wall who is blithely writing out a prescription for some potentially deadly and certainly addictive drug to push down the gullet of some poor man, woman, or child who has fallen into his clutches. These legally sanctioned drug pushers—and that's all they are—know that they are frauds, know that nothing they are writing prescriptions for will ever "cure" anyone in their clutches of anything.

The so-called "antidepressants," just for example, have as a side effect "suicidal or homicidal ideation." They were never designed to do anything but to make men tractable, quiet, and untroublesome. Yet these witch-doctors hand them out like candy. And the suicide rates climb, and they don't care. They always claim that it wasn't the drug, it was the underlying condition. Of course it was.

Virtually every single mass murderer in the last 50 or more years—leaving out, for the moment, Muslim terrorists, which are covered in a later chapter—has been in the hands of a psychiatrist, and has been on one or more psychiatric drugs. Drug companies like Eli Lilly pay obscene amounts of money to keep this fact out of public records and news reports, but on their hands is the blood of uncounted thousands of victims of suicide and mass murder.

Yet our government actually keeps these doctoral-degree ghouls on the payroll to guide the "treatment" of grieving survivors of the very holocausts that the doctoral-degree ghouls themselves create. And don't look now, but they also sit like vultures on trees over every single one of our elected and appointed officials—including the ones with the codes for nuclear weapons.

Once Wundt and his army of man-has-no-soul sadists took over the once benign field of "psychology," that left religion and mysticism to rule alone the kingdom of mystery, the unexplainable, things that go boomp in the night, infinity, the afterlife, and all the vast body of data and evidence and records of phenomena that the physical sciences carefully tiptoe around, or hire shoddy lounge-lizard materialist stage magicians such as "The Amazing Randi" to "debunk." (It's a pity that "The Amazing Randi" turned out to be merely one more amazing liar and fraud, who lived his entire life as a lie, carefully hiding the fact that he was disposed, like Shaftesbury and Locke, "to serve and assist the Pleasures and Debauches of *Men that way inclined.*" Oh, well.)

There's another important region of the kingdom of religions, though, one that might be most significant of all, and that is morals. Morals, East and West, have been set down and passed on as part of religious teachings, and for most of man's civilized history, those moral values guided not only day-to-day human intercourse, but ruled the rulers. Moral codes derived from spiritual convictions were the most fundamental guidelines for civilized forms of government, and served as the primary constraint on all rulers and leaders to respect the unique unequaled individuality of each of the governed.

So what, really, are "morals"? Who, today, are the keepers of "morals"? What has John Locke done to the world's ideas of morals? Who is to decide what is moral or immoral?

8. John Locke's Political Anarchy and Steal-It Theory of Property
Shepherding a Flock of Shepherds

Before daring out again into the tar pit of John Locke's political lunacy, I'm going to establish some walkways over it created with solid planks of fundamental definitions, which are mine. They may not be yours. They may not be blessed by the Holiest of Holies "experts" on Lockean Lunacy and Political Theory, but frankly, having seen some of their "analysis" (some of which I have shared, and more of which I will share with you in a moment), I don't give a damn. Here are the basic definitions in use in this chapter:

> **Moral codes** are forms of *law* to govern conduct, issued by decree of some authority, often religious. They are themselves *laws* in the sense of this definition of "law" from Merriam-Webster: "a binding custom or practice of a community: a rule of conduct or action prescribed or formally recognized as binding or enforced by a controlling authority."

> **Civil laws** are, in essence, decreed or legislated *moral codes,* but issued and enforced by a political or governmental authority, and applying broadly to all people who are subject to that political or governmental authority, regardless of any other moral codes in use by any subset of those people.

103

All politics and government distill down to one and only
one thing: *the right and power to make and enforce laws.*

That is far too simple—and inarguable—a fact to be lent any
credence whatsoever by any school, of any description, at any level,
anywhere on the face of the earth today. To accept it would be to
crumble into dust and ruin tens of thousands of institutions and
careers and bloated salaries devoted entirely to making it as complex
and mysterious—and, really, sometimes as hysterically funny—as
possible, with tens of millions of pages pounded out in theses and
counter-theses and journal papers and books and newspapers and
magazines, a daily flood from an infinite wellspring of madness and
confusion.

Down in all that flood of sticky ink somewhere you'll find John
Locke's theories on government. And tar. Lots of tar. We're going to
get to that Lockean tar pit of "politics" momentarily, because our
entire system of government in the United States, and the systems
of many governments in the world, are built on top of it, right now,
today.

But the simple and inescapable fact is that all politics, all
government of any description, whether local, regional, national,
global, secular, or theological, over any group of any size, from
familial to international, is nothing whatsoever other than *the right
and power to make and enforce laws.*

It doesn't matter one gnat's breath whether such right and power
purportedly derives from one or more gods on high (in which the
laws are synonymous with "morals"), or from the "consent" of the
governed, or from having the biggest and baddest army or weapon
available, or from having the most material wealth, or from being
mommy or daddy: *all* politics, *all* systems of government and control
of a group, any group, of any size, shape, or description, throughout
all of history and now and forevermore, consists solely of gaining and
maintaining *the right and power to make and enforce laws.*

Moses came down from the mount and handed out *laws* that he
said came from Yahweh/El himself.

Mohammed went into a cave and came out claiming to have a book of *laws* from Allah/Yahweh/El himself.

Most such religion-based *laws*, which are viewed as and commonly called *moral codes*, are enforced not by force or arms or police, but by peer pressure or threats of eternal damnation for violation—though in some theocracies, where the moral code *is* the civil law, as in Islam, some violations are punishable by mutilation or death.

Many existing civil laws have evolved into being as civil laws after starting out as moral codes.

All monarchies, whether elective or hereditary, whether of king, queen, emperor, pharaoh, khan, caliph, tribal chief, or any other regal, royal, or sole-leader title, exist solely because that monarch has achieved *the power to make and enforce laws,* whether that power was attained by force of arms or by the force a mother pushing in a labor of birth.

All dictatorships, however they arise, exist solely because the dictator has gained, usually through force of arms, *the right and power to make and enforce laws.*

When the power to make and enforce laws resides in several branches of government—such as in the United States' system of three branches—it's exactly the same power and authority, but distributed. In the case of the United States, the Legislative branch creates the laws; the Executive and Judicial branches enforce the laws. (Yes, the Judicial branch sometimes must "interpret" the law, but that is merely a sub-function of its enforcement.) Even in this system, the Legislative must work with the Executive—specifically, the President—to have proposed legislation become realized law, because the President must approve laws passed by Congress, in most cases, for those laws to take effect. Sometimes in government and in business such laws or official guiding codes are referred to as *policy*—which traces back to similar roots as the word *politics*.

The word "police" comes to us from roots that also give us "politics" and "policy." All police forces, of whatever organizational structure or nature—including military organizations—exist as a sub-function of, and under control of the authority that has, *the right and power to make and enforce laws.*

An interesting illustration of some of these principles happened in England to its monarchy. Various forms of Parliament began to enter the picture in 1215 when a group of locals grabbed the English king by his ermine lapels at Runnymede and pinned his ears back, resulting in the Magna Carta. Still, ultimate authority vested in the king, more or less—that itself a topic of sometimes-violent disagreement amongst "experts," but more or less.

Things changed forever in 1641, though, when the English Parliament frantically created the Militia Bill, electing themselves as the official "creators" of an army. Creation grants authority. In any "sole mystical creator" doctrine, such as the Judeo-Christian scripture, *creation* is *authority.*

It therefore should be little cause for wonder that scarcely eight years after the Militia Bill, at the end of January 1649, King Charles I was beheaded—where not very far away from the site of the beheading sat a wan, asthmatic student who took alternate doses of culture and canings from the headmaster at Westminster. His name was John Locke.

Creation grants authority, and creation of armies backs it up. In spades.

But if Morals Are Laws, and Laws Are Morals, What Are Ethics?

If you want to step onto another merry-go-round to nowhere—one not directly built by John Locke, but certainly contributed to by him—just go to any dictionary and look up the definitions of "moral(s)" and "ethic(s)." Let's look at this spinning cyclotron—from a safe distance. First, here are the relevant definitions from Dictionary.com, which is based on the Random House Dictionary (bold emphasis added):

> **moral**
> *adjective:* of, relating to, or concerned with the principles or **rules of right conduct** or the distinction between right and wrong; **ethical**
> *noun:* morals, **principles** or habits with respect to **right or wrong conduct.**

> **ethics**
> *noun:* the body of **moral principles** or values governing or distinctive of a particular culture or group; a complex of **moral precepts** held or **rules of conduct** followed by an individual

Surely Merriam-Webster will stop our heads from spinning round and round:

> **moral**
> *adjective:* of or relating to **principles** of **right and wrong** in behavior: **ethical**
> *noun:* morals, moral practices or teachings: **modes of conduct**
>
> **ethics**
> *noun:* the discipline dealing with what is **good and bad** and with **moral** duty and obligation

If you need to take a walk and clear your head, I understand, and it certainly would be a good idea before we get to the tar pit of Lockean views on government, but there really is a simple difference between *morals* and *ethics*:

Morals—and official civil laws—are the rules of conduct handed down to you *by another or others,* whether they came from a parent, a school superintendent, a city council, a dictator, a king, a congress, a prophet, or a god. If you consider them to be correct morals to guide your conduct, then you have subscribed to them in some way, either through domination, or willing agreement, or mere acceptance without question, or desire to be part of the group—however large or small—that shares that set of moral codes or laws, based on acceptance of the authority that handed them down.

Ethics consist of your own personal decisions to follow or depart from such externally established, other-determined codes of conduct. Ethics are based on your own integrity, observation, and contemplation of what will result in the greatest good—not just for yourself, but also for those whose lives your decisions and actions affect, such as family, neighbors, community, workplace, nation, or all of mankind.

It must be mentioned in passing that there can exist *ethical codes*—which are **not** *moral codes* because *ethical codes* cannot be enforced; they can be subscribed to solely by one's own self-determined choice as a point of honor. The old codes of chivalry, and many codes of etiquette, are more along the lines of *ethical codes* than moral codes.

One problem with trying to rely on "morals" as the sole guide for responsible conduct is that there are probably, right now, today, at least a thousand or more moral codes and "laws"—civil, religious, and tribal—swirling around you in this world. Some of them are thousands of years old. Many of them are sensible and even ethical to follow, but others—such as "moral codes" that sanction the wholesale slaughter of human beings in acts of terror—are thoroughly destructive and reprehensible to any person with a shred of responsibility and *ethics*.

When conflicting moral codes are crammed or forced together into any group of any size or description, from family to nation, hostilities are inevitable.

So moral codes decidedly are *not* "created equal." And that, regrettably, brings us face-to-face again with John Locke and the madhouse of Lockean lunacy on what "government" is and should be, because government—all government—exists solely in terms of *the right and power to make and enforce laws.*

The "Experts" Chime in on Locke's Treatises on Government

John Locke famously—or infamously; depends on who you talk to—wrote *Two Treatises on Government.* Earlier in his life, while busy getting himself into the slave trading business, he had written *Two Tracts on Government,* in which he pontificated decidedly on the side of the divine right of kings. It almost got published in 1661—but Locke pulled the plug on it at the last minute. (The work never saw the light of day until it was exhumed in 1967, and is largely ignored by the disciples of Locke. There's no need to get hung up on the different titles of these very different works—the Tracts and the Treatises—other than to keep them differentiated. Locke didn't give any name at all to many of his works; the names we know some of them by are "names" thunk up by Locke's fanboys.)

Later in his life, after writing but not publishing the *Two **Tracts** on Government,* Locke did a complete flip-flop, and churned out *Two **Treatises** on Government,* condemning any "divine right" of kings, insisting that governance should only be by the consent of the governed. That's where he informed us that we all are "equal and independent." For our initial address to *Two Treatises on Government,* we're going to turn to an entire herd of Locke's fanboys—the Holiest of Holies in the Deep Dark Secrets of the Lockean Canon: the PhD'ed experts. And here's why we're going to turn them loose on it:

John Locke is the to the English language what waterboarding is to water. If it can be said in five words, he will use fifty or five hundred—and not to say it, but to jabber around it, to pose florid self-serving questions about it, to drop sly hints and innuendo. This is more than merely the ornamental style of prose common to 17th-century English; Locke perfected the black art of sophistry through a brutal abuse of the Socratic method that is so monotonous in its singsong pace, so couched in generalities, so fly-blown with extraneous commas and semicolons and rhetorical questions, so mincing and circuitous, so covertly self-contradictory that it works like a swinging watch on a chain to put readers into a hypnotic trance so they will believe he actually said something.

He is so incomprehensible that if you read two different "authorities" on Locke, you will get at least 14 different and differing "interpretations" of his scream-inducing scratchings—because "all the authorities" (apologies to Bob Dylan) feel compelled to tediously, tiresomely quote and agree with or disagree with other "authorities" in order to firmly establish their status as "authorities"—not that any of them make any more sense than Locke himself.

If you actually have read Locke's original works—rather than do what most do, which is read *about* Locke and his works—you damned well deserve a diploma, not because you learned something, but on the same basis as one of the old tests for witches: If you were thrown into a deep pond, bound around with heavy stones, and you sank and drowned rather than floated to the top, then you deserved to be pronounced innocent of being a witch. (Or, rather, you deserved to be pronounced innocent of *having been* a witch. R.I.P.)

If you're ever given the choice of reading the works of Locke or taking a root canal without benefit of Novocain, I heartily recommend choosing the root canal. It will be faster and less painful, and you probably won't go into a coma more than once.

Charles Lutwidge Dodgson—who you probably know very well by his pen name, Lewis Carroll—studied and worked at John Locke's old alma mater, Christ Church, Oxford, and I cannot be dissuaded from believing in my heart that his depiction of the howlingly mad Hatter's Tea Party is a faithful re-creation of the types of "disputations" that John Locke and his cronies were given to. Those gab-fests must have been very much like what we're about to encounter in considering excerpts from an article published by the Stanford Encyclopedia of Philosophy, called "Locke's Political Philosophy." It is an in-depth "expert" analysis of Locke's *Two Treatises on Government*, authored by man with a string of impressive credentials named Alex Tuckness, PhD. He describes himself thus:

> I received my PhD in Politics from Princeton, my Masters in Political Thought and Intellectual History from Cambridge University, and my bachelors degree in Political Science from the University of Chicago.

We've already established, in an earlier chapter, just how prestigious Stanford University is, and here we have the combined weight, force, authority, and majesty not only of Stanford, but of Princeton, Cambridge, and Chicago universities delivered into our questing and quivering hands. But we have far, far more than even that, because Dr. Tuckness has brought a thundering herd of fellow experts along with him to analyze Locke's major work on government.

The article from Dr. Tuckness and friends says right at the outset that Locke "is among the most influential political philosophers of the modern period." Well! They should know! Then what wisdom must be hidden in the depths of this Lockean pit? What have all these brilliant, learned, authoritatively educated men and women found by diving headlong into this dark, sticky philosophical pool of Locke's legacy called *Two Treatises on Government?* I must humbly stand aside and let them tell us themselves all about the true meaning and purpose of politics and government, Locke style (some bold emphasis added):

> Perhaps **the most central concept** in Locke's political philosophy is his theory of **natural law** and **natural rights** ...

I'm sorry; forgive me for the interruption; I said I will stand aside, and I will, but first I simply must emphasize, lest it be lost, this *crucial, pivotal* point made by the good Dr. Tuckness: "the **most central concept** in Locke's **political philosophy** is his **theory of natural law** and **natural rights.**" Hold onto that thought as though it were the safety bar on a roller coaster, because here we go again. Strictly for the purposes of analysis and commentary, I am selecting only the most germane excerpts, here, concerning Locke's vitally important "natural law" and "natural rights":

> It must be admitted that Locke did not treat the topic of natural law as systematically as one might like ...
>
> With respect to the grounds and content of natural law, Locke is not completely clear ...
>
> Locke clearly wants to avoid the implication that the content of natural law is arbitrary ...
>
> With respect to the specific content of natural law, Locke never provides a comprehensive statement of what it requires ...
>
> Another point of contestation has to do with the extent to which Locke thought natural law could, in fact, be known ...
>
> Both [Leo] Strauss and Peter Laslett, though very different in their interpretations of Locke generally, see Locke's theory of natural law as filled with contradictions ...
>
> Strauss infers ... that the contradictions exist to show the attentive reader that Locke does not really believe in natural law at all. Laslett, more conservatively, simply says that Locke ...
>
> Even though Locke thought natural law could be known apart from special revelation, he saw no contradiction in God playing a part in the argument ...
>
> Locke avoided this problem because consistency with natural law was one of the criteria he used when deciding the proper interpretation of Biblical passages ...
>
> Locke's concept of the state of nature has been interpreted by commentators in a variety of ways ...
>
> There is considerable disagreement as to how these factors are to be understood ...

Would you like one lump or two with your tea? Treacle? Lemon? A touch of tar? Is this matter of "natural law" all clear to you so far? I certainly hope so, because we've been instructed that it is *central* to Locke's *political philosophy*. But did Dr. Dormouse—I mean, Tuckness—just say there is "considerable disagreement?" Between the "authorities," the "experts" of academia? Surely not! Almost every statehouse standing in the world is built on the foundation of this bog, so *surely* these most learned, scholarly men and women from only the most learned, scholarly (and, by the way, did I mention prestigious?) institutions, are going to deliver to us some solid, incontrovertible wisdom on politics and government from the meticulous mind of John Locke. *Surely* they will:

> More scholars have adopted the view of Dunn, Tully, and Ashcraft that it is natural law, not natural rights, that is primary ...
>
> Simmons takes a position similar to the latter group, but claims ...
>
> Brian Tienrey questions whether one needs to prioritize natural law or natural right ...
>
> There have been some attempts to find a compromise between these positions. Michael Zuckert's version of the Straussian position acknowledges ...
>
> Zuckert still questions the sincerity of Locke's theism, but thinks that Locke does develop a position ...
>
> Strauss, and many of his followers ... point out that Locke defended a hedonist theory of human motivation ...
>
> Straussians make Locke's theory relevant by claiming that the theological dimensions of his thought are primarily rhetorical ...
>
> Adam Seagrave ... argues that the contradiction between Locke's claim that human beings are owned by God and that human beings own themselves ...
>
> Many scholars reject this position. Yolton, Colman, Ashcraft, Grant, Simmons, Tuckness and others all argue that there is nothing strictly inconsistent in Locke's admission ...
>
> Herzog makes Locke an intellectualist by grounding our obligation to obey God ...

Wait, wait, wait: I'm sorry, I almost nodded off into a coma, but did he just say "God"? We're "owned by God" and have an "obligation to obey God"? I thought we were talking about civil government. And, well—which "god"? Is this the same "god" that supposedly created us all as "equal"? Locke has already told us quite emphatically that: "Men in all religions have *equally* strong persuasions, and every one must judge for himself; nor can any one judge for another." But one god, Yahweh, commands "Thou shalt not kill," and another god, Allah, commands "Kill them [unbelievers] wherever you find them." So which of these "gods" is more *equal* than the other? Or are both of those gods really El, which would mean he was just two-faced? Hello? Experts?

And poor reader: Are you there? Have *you* slipped into a coma yet? No? Well, obviously, then, you haven't had quite enough "enlightenment" about government, Lockean style, from the High Priests of Academia, and about just how damned important this "natural law" issue is for you to understand in understanding Locke. Take deep breaths:

> To understand Locke's position on the ground of natural law it must be situated within a larger debate in natural law theory that predates Locke, the so-called "voluntarism-intellectualism," or "voluntarist-rationalist" debate ...
> Herzog makes Locke an intellectualist ...
> A second option, suggested by Simmons, is simply to take Locke as a voluntarist ...
> A third option, suggested by Tuckness (and implied by Grant), is to treat the question of voluntarism as having two different parts ...

Okay, stop. Just stop right there. Did I understand correctly that all of this "voluntarism-intellectualism" jibber-jabber amongst these academic "experts" and "authorities" is predicated on the premise that it is part of "a larger debate in natural law theory that *predates* Locke"? Well, that is curious indeed. No, it's beyond curious: it shreds the space-time continuum. It puts John Locke into a Time Machine in the 17th century and launches him over 200 years into the future. Why?

Because according to *every dictionary that can be found and consulted*—including the Oxford dictionary, from the very institution where Locke was schooled—the term "voluntarist" or "volunarism" *didn't even exist* until 1838, and was not used in the *philosophic sense* until 1896. Locke died in 1704, so he had been dead as a hammer for 134 years before the word was even used at all, and he had been moldering in the churchyard of High Laver in Essex for 192 years before the term was ever used in a *philosophical context*. It is truly metaphysical, then, downright paranormal, that philosophers *predating* Locke could have been churning up drawing rooms with debates on the subject.

Reader? Poor reader. I tried my best, in good faith, to warn you, but ... Oh, look: the experts are talking again:

> Others, such as Dunn, take Locke to be of only limited relevance to contemporary politics ...

Oh! Say it isn't so!

> A number of authors, such as Simmons and Vernon, have tried to separate the foundations of Locke's argument from other aspects of it ...

I idly wonder how, exactly, they separate tar.

> Simmons, for example, argues that Locke's thought is over-determined ...
> Waldron, in his most recent work on Locke, explores the opposite claim ...
> Simmons presents an important challenge to this view ...
> According to Strauss, Locke presents the state of nature as a factual description of what the earliest society is like ...
> A complementary interpretation is made by John Dunn ...
> None of these interpretations claims that Locke's state of nature is only a thought experiment, in the way Kant and Rawls are normally thought to use the concept ...
> Locke's treatment of property is generally thought to be among his most important contributions in political thought, but it is also one of the aspects of his thought that has been most heavily criticized ...

As they sink, burbling and gurgling, going round and round, down and down into the tar, the tea cups rattling, let's remove our hats—here on solid ground—for a moment of silence. And right about now, a little silence would be most welcomed indeed. Maybe they will bubble up to the surface if we need them again. Meanwhile, given that with their last gurgle they mentioned Locke's "treatment of property" being "among his most important contributions in political thought" ...

John Locke's Theory of Property Creates Capitalism—and Socialism

You probably think that the subheading immediately above has to be a joke, but it is absolutely true—however frightening a prospect that should be, and is.

History.com has a page titled "John Locke—Facts & Summary," and it states the following:

> Locke ... developed a definition of property as the product of a person's labor that would be foundational for both Adam Smith's capitalism and Karl Marx's socialism.

You may feel the need to read that sentence again, perhaps several times. This statement is stunning simply because it peels back a scab on the essence of Locke's contagious madness that has raced around the globe for over 300 years like a pandemic plague, infecting everything and everyone it comes in contact with. In exactly the same way that Lockean lunacy donned the robes of a mysterious nonexistent "Creator" to guide the hand of Thomas Jefferson and appear as creationism in the *Declaration of Independence,* then donned the plumes of a paganistic parrot to sit on the shoulder of Charles Darwin as he navigated the globe, developing a godless theory of materialistic evolution, so this virulent disease of Lockeanism seeped into the embryonic tissues of Adam Smith's capitalism being gestated in England, then erupted as congenital lesions oozing socialism from Karl Marx.

John Locke postulated socialism and its uglier sister communism by claiming that everyone everywhere owned everything equally:

> God ... hath given the world to men in common ... .

It's just that blatant. It's just that simple. That's where Locke starts, and any child of 6 could understand that Locke insists that everybody owns everything. Period. (As we're going to see soon, Locke stole that idea.) And of course it only can be tar from there on down.

But then Locke spun around in the same treatise, and like a two-faced god issued another proclamation postulating capitalism—but as thievery. Locke granted his *uberequal* man-animal a simple means of individual ownership: theft from the other *uberequal* owners:

> Whatsoever then he removes out of the state that nature hath provided ... [he] thereby makes it his property.

In short: if you can steal it from everybody else by any means, it's yours. But Locke was familiar with theft as a way of life, having thieved most of his ideas. He makes his Theft Theory of Property crystal clear—clear enough, you would think, for even someone with a PhD to understand it:

> It [anything at all] being by him removed from the common state nature hath placed it in, it hath by this labour something annexed to it, that excludes the common right of other men.

We never find out what this mysterious "something" is that's suddenly "annexed to" the stolen property—just as we never find out from Locke what "natural law" and "natural rights" are—but apparently this "annexed" *thing* has mystical exclusionary powers that annihilate, nullify, and negate any right anyone else has to that stolen thing, even though it previously belonged to them, too. This mystical "something" might be Medusa. It might be Tinker Bell. It might be fairy dust. Or, I know: It must be Synergy! But that's commerce and property in a nutshell according to Locke: theft by any means, redefined as "labour." And your sons and daughters will never get out of a college or university alive without having this drilled into them as brilliant philosophy. Speaking of colleges and universities, I see a hand being raised in the tar. I think our experts want to bubble and gurgle a bit about this subject of property, capitalism, and socialism:

> One interpretation, advanced by C. B. Macpherson, sees Locke as a defender of unrestricted capitalist accumulation ...
> Macpherson's understanding of Locke has been criticized ...
> Alan Ryan argued that since property for Locke includes life and liberty as well as estate ... even those without land could ...
> James Tully attacked Macpherson's interpretation by pointing out that ...
>
> Robert Nozick criticized this argument with his famous example of mixing tomato juice one rightfully owns ...
> Sreenivasan has defended Tully's argument against Waldron's response ...
> Waldron claims that, contrary to Macpherson, Tully, and others, Locke did not recognize a sufficiency condition ...
> Simmons presents a still different synthesis. He sides with Waldron and against Tully and Sreenivasan ...
> Nozick takes Locke to be a libertarian, with the government having no right to take property ...

> At the other extreme, Tully thinks that, by the time government is formed, land is already scarce ...
> Waldron's view is in between these ...

Oh, do, please, shut up and have another cup of tar. I mean tea. While we're on this subject of property, though, and while the "experts" are trying to throttle each other, we can't leave it without at least a brief address to:

The Private Property Abolition Acts of 1964 and 1968

If you live in the United States and think you own a piece of real estate, either a residence or a business, the joke's on you. All ownership of such property in the United States was transferred to the federal government in 1964, reinforced in 1968, with two brilliant pieces of legislative legerdemain having the wonderfully deceptive titles of the Civil Rights Act of 1964 and the Civil Rights Act of 1968.

While they certainly made needed reforms in government institutions, one of the main covert purposes was to nullify ownership of private property. In fact, it gave the federal government more actual hands-on co-ownership in every piece of private property in the United States than any tyrannical monarch ever had over his subjects.

The very definition of ownership, in a legal sense, is "one with the right to exclusive use, control, or possession of property." *Black's Law Dictionary* defines it as "the complete dominion, title, or proprietary right in a thing or claim."

The U.S. federal government now has the right and dominion to tell you how you can and cannot use any business property in the United States, who you must cater your business to, and exact standards to which you must comply if you choose to liquidate or sell such property, business or residential. Failure to meet any of the owner's demands—and the federal government is the owner, by exact definitions—can result in severe penalties, including fines and even jail time. Only the owner of a business or property could have such dominion over it.

And you think you're the "owner." By the way, did you *consent* to giving up that much control and ownership in what you thought was your property?

Consenting Adults—The Alleged Consent of the Governed

If John Locke ever had an original thought in his life, I've never found anyone who has found it, and his "consent of the governed" doctrine is no different. He treated intellectual property as he did all property: he stole it when it pleased him, and he added some "labour" to it by perverting it enough to disguise its real ownership and source.

That lack of originality, of course, is consistent with John Locke's assertion that none of us is capable, ever, of an original thought, so can only cobble together material sensory impressions rushing in on us from the external world. It is a pitiable, pathetic state to consider, and there is little wonder why he was sickly all his life, but apparently that is the state that John Locke was in, because that's exactly how he created his own works: Like someone shoplifting at a Salvation Army store, he would pick this bauble here, that knick-knack there, a cracked saucer here, a sweater missing a button there, then he would sneak out with them under his coat and assemble them all together into a sort of Frankenstein monster of philosophical bits and pieces—stolen, of course, but also twisted or mauled into something unrecognizable. This weird idea of "consent of the governed" is one of the bizarre bits and pieces Locke stole.

H. R. Fox Bourne, in his biography of Locke, hints at one of the places and means by which Locke almost certainly found some of the key principles that he would later steal, twist, mangle, and present as his own. It was while Locke was a student the Westminster School in London—which was only a short walk from where King Charles I was tried and then beheaded:

> He [Locke] was within hearing of the noise, if not an actual eye-witness, of the exploit for which the 30th of January, [1649], will ever be one of the most memorable days in English history, the day on which a king professing to reign by divine right was executed in Whitehall Palace Yard as a traitor to the commonwealth entrusted to his keeping; and, during the two or three years before and the two or three years after that great crisis, he [Locke] was very near to the centre of the English Rebellion, and must have heard much, and doubtless thought much, about all these strange and solemn doings. The great political events of the time must have conveyed many

> memorable lessons to the schoolboy whose quiet cloisters were in such immediate proximity to the very spring and centre of their action. By listeners in peaceful nooks and corners the sounds that reach them from the bustling outside world are sometimes more plainly heard than by those among the crowd whose voices help to make the turmoil.

That "English Rebellion" Bourne speaks of that no doubt "conveyed many memorable lessons" to Locke had been made rebellious indeed by a man named John Lilburne, who at the time of the kingly beheading was in the Tower of London—also not terribly far from where Locke was being schooled—because of his revolutionary writings and activities. He and groups such as the Levellers and the Diggers were spreading all over London some of the exact, precise concepts that years later would turn up in John Locke's writing—including the "consent" doctrine, which fools today attribute fawningly to Locke. There's no intention here to write yet another version of the many histories of groups and individuals involved in this time of political upheaval in England, but at least a brief annotated pre-Ashley/Shaftesbury timeline of Locke's student life, and some of the central ideas that were raging all over London at the time, helps to expose Locke for the plagiarist he was.

1 c. March c. 1646
Approximate time when John Locke is sent to Westminster School in London. He is about 14 years old. (Bourne)

28 October 1647
The "Putney Debates" begin, arranged to discuss constitutional changes to the ruling of England in the wake of the civil war. The debates result partly in publication of the first version of a series of famous documents called "An Agreement of the People" (short title). The debates include such statements as "every Man that is to live under a Government ought first **by his own Consent** to put himself under that Government." A group called the Levellers is involved in these debates, and instrumental in creating the

"Agreement of the People." They also are champions of a concept that all people have fundamental "natural" rights.

This "consent" mandate is the exact concept of "consent" that Locke would trot out over 40 years later—twisted—in his *Two Treatises on Government,* which concept many fanboy "experts" treat as though it were some startling new revelation Locke had received from on high. Locke clearly picked up other pieces of his political philosophy from the Levellers, too, as will soon be shown.

30 January 1649
King Charles I is beheaded not far from where John Locke is living as a student, at Westminster School.

31 January 1649
As part of a prayer read in the House of Commons the day after the execution of King Charles I, a revered and well known theologian named John Owen submits into the Parliamentary record his essay entitled "Of **toleration**; and the duty of the magistrate about religion." In it, Owen argues that civil authorities should not punish people based on their religious beliefs and practices unless those activities disrupt the civil peace and safety.

This "toleration" creed is the exact same concept that later will appear, expanded, in John Locke's essays and letters on "toleration." Locke will write those *after* he becomes a student at Christ Church, Oxford— where *this very same John Owen* will be dean of Christ Church college and Vice Chancellor of Oxford University when Locke arrives, and will be very well known by Locke. There can be no slightest question that Locke picked up this idea of religious "toleration" from Owen, tucked it into his vest, and saved it until he could make it sound like it was his own.

1 April 1649

A group that comes to be called the "Diggers" begins digging up the land and planting crops on St. George's Hill in Surrey, England. A pamphlet being widely circulated by and about them at the time says in part: "In the beginning of Time, the great **Creator Reason,** made the Earth to be a **Common Treasury**, to preserve Beasts, Birds, Fishes, and Man, the lord that was to govern this Creation; for Man had Domination given to him, over the Beasts, Birds, and Fishes; but **not one word** was spoken in the beginning, **That one branch of mankind should rule over another.**"

Some of these central concepts from the Diggers turn up later almost verbatim in several of Locke's works, including the concept of equality, of "Reason" being the will of the "Creator" and the "law of nature," and of everything in the Earth being a "Common Treasury" belonging equally to everyone.

1 May 1649

Leaders of the revolutionary group the Levellers have been jailed in the Tower of London, but from their imprisonment they manage to get issued, printed, and widely circulated a new version of the "Agreement of the People," this version having the title, "An Agreement of the Free People of England, Tendered as a Peace-Offering to this Distressed Nation." It is written by John Lilburne, William Walwyn, Thomas Prince, and Richard Overton. It calls for such civil liberties as "universal vote, the right to silence in the dock [freedom from self incrimination], equal parliamentary constituencies, **everyone being equal under the law**," and "the right not to be conscripted into the army." (Quoted descriptions from the Constitution Society, http://www. constitution.org/eng/agreepeo.htm) It also calls for **freedom of religious faith and worship, without civil "Lawes, Oaths, or Covenants, whereby to compell by penalties."**

Once again, we have here concepts swirling all around Locke, as a student in London, that later will be knotted and glued and riveted into Locke's own rickety erector-set constructions of tortured syntax—although often with hopelessly contradictory concepts stolen from other sources.

These sources listed in this brief timeline are merely by example—but it conclusively shows relationships in Locke's zeitgeist that no other analysis anywhere has revealed with clarity. In addition to these, Locke cherry-picked, as was convenient to his loopy whims, from sources as diverse as the Bible, Thomas More's *Utopia,* Thomas Hobbes's *Leviathan,* Richard Hooker's *Of the Lawes of Ecclesiastical Politie,* René Descartes, Saint Thomas Aquinas, Robert Sanderson, William Barclay, Plato, Aristotle, and lord only knows how many more. Of course it's sensible that anyone assaying to embark on the philosophy of politics would gain a familiarity with earlier thinkers and wisdom, but Locke's perverse art was to steal from them, often without any attribution at all, and cram conflicting and contradictory ingredients together into— Well, into tar.

Part of what the 1 May 1649 "Agreement of the Free People" included was an insistence that the people be governed by elected representatives, which the document described as being "according to naturall [sic] right." Years later, John Locke will unabashedly steal this—lock (pun unavoidable), stock, and natural right—without the decency of even a slight acknowledgment or thanks to Lilburne and the Levellers. This tar bed of "natural rights," though, is so sticky, deadly, that it is the subject of the next chapter.

John Lilburne, who earned the nickname "Freeborn John," became popular enough with the public that when he was found *not guilty* of treason at a trial held in London's Guildhall, on 24 October of 1649, the shouting of celebration held up the ability of the court to officially end the session. He had gone on trial for treason because he and his fellow Levellers had the courage of their convictions and had stood up publicly for what they believed. In that respect, and in many of their beliefs, they foreshadowed the coming of the

Founding Fathers of the United States, and the resulting *Declaration of Independence* and *Constitution*. All of this political intrigue and uproar with Lilburne and the Levellers was happening within easy walking distance from where Locke was a student, and he would have had to be deaf and blind to miss it. He didn't miss it. He carefully tucked it all away to plagiarize as his own later—when it was safer. He was ever too cowardly and sycophantic to put his principles or his neck on the line.

1 c. May 1651

Leviathan, a book of political philosophy by Thomas Hobbes, is published in London. In it, Hobbes postulates a **"state of nature"** that he describes as a war "of every man against every man." He opines that life is "solitary, poor, nasty, brutish, and short" unless men have "a common power to keep them all in awe." Hobbes also maintains that part of this "state of nature" is that every man has a **"right to all things."** Another vital concept in the book is that a sovereign can rule only because **the majority of his subjects have consented to his rule.**

It is breathtaking to come fully to grips with all the concepts that John Locke lifted, with no conscience of depth or depth of conscience, from his contemporaries. He must have had a copy of *Leviathan* open (with text in it probably underlined) when he wrote some of his copy-cat "philosophy." Locke's entire "state of nature" dogma is barely even reworded from Hobbes. Isaac Newton saw through this when he accused Locke, ever so correctly, of being a "Hobbist" after Locke's *Essay Concerning Human Understanding* had been published.

Leviathan advocates for a monarchy (one would hope a benign one) and public submission to such a sovereign, and Locke's *Two Treatises on Government* are largely viewed as advocating against such complete power vested in a sovereign, but in fact the *first* work that John Locke wrote about government was his *Two **Tracts** on Government*—never published until several centuries later—and it almost could be called *Leviathan Lite*.

In it, Locke not only advocates for a sovereign, but grants that such a sovereign should have full power to "lawfully impose and determine" practices of religious worship. It shouldn't escape notice that Locke wrote that work in 1660, about nine years after *Leviathan*—and almost immediately after Charles II had been seated to the throne of England, beginning the Restoration of monarchy after the chaos of Cromwell's reign-that-was-not-a-reign, known as the Interregnum. As usual, Locke was playing to power, but even then he chickened out of having his work published. He wouldn't do his Jekyll-and-Hyde flip-flop to his *Two **Treatises** on Government* theories for about another 30 years—and that only after he had been involved, to some still-undetermined degree, with Shaftesbury in a treasonous conspiracy to assassinate King Charles II and his brother, James, Duke of York.

In any case, this "consent" doctrine and dogma is a two-edged sword, an ambiguity, all in addition to being sort of a penetrating glimpse into the obvious.

Its ambiguity arises from the definition of "consent," which can mean, almost equally, willing agreement—or merely compliance or acquiescence. Here, from Dictionary.com:

> **consent:** permission, approval, or agreement; compliance; acquiescence

So to say that the governed, in any system of governance, gives their "consent" is to say essentially nothing. The fact of their being governed, rather than governing, pretty much demonstrates their consent. Whether it is willing, or enthusiastic, or happy, or grumbling, or reluctant, or apathetic "consent" makes all the difference in the concept of "consent." Throughout all of time and history, people who were not enslaved have mostly had options to pack up and go somewhere else, or have had some means of making known to governing rulers or bodies their discontent. Rulers throughout history have not all been despots or tyrants or sadists; most have wanted, within their own zeitgeists and traditions, to make the lives of their subjects as good as possible. In some ancient systems, even the so-called slaves and servants were given freedoms and benefits as human beings, and held a close devotion to their masters.

That is no praise of or case for the practice of slavery in any form; it simply is a fact of history. There has long been a very fuzzy and foggy line between the concepts of servant, serf, and slave, and there are excellent arguments that income tax is merely serfdom and slavery renamed. But that's another book.

John Locke, though—that great and renowned "father of liberalism" who in fact was a slave trader—condoned and justified slavery right up to his last breath, and said so in his *Two Tracts on Government:*

> There is [a] sort of servants, which by a peculiar name we call slaves, who being captives taken in a just war, are by the right of nature subjected to the absolute dominion and arbitrary power of their masters. These men having, as I say, forfeited their lives, and with it their liberties, and lost their estates; and being in the state of slavery, not capable of any property, cannot in that state be considered as any part of civil society; the chief end whereof is the preservation of property.

If that doesn't seal his hideous duplicitous hypocrisy for you, Locke came along *in the same document* and laid down the law on the vital necessity of "consent":

> For no government can have a right to obedience from a people who have not freely consented to it; which they can never be supposed to do, till either they are put in a full state of liberty to choose their government and governors, or at least till they have such standing laws, to which they have by themselves or their representatives given their free consent; and also till they are allowed their due property, which is so to be proprietors of what they have, that nobody can take away any part of it without their own consent, without which, men under any government are not in the state of freemen, but are direct slaves under the force of war.

So we all can only try to imagine how every great civilization for thousands of years—civilizations producing boundless wisdom and art and culture—somehow managed to crawl along on their bellies, as "direct slaves under the force of war," without the benefit of an asthmatic sissified bookworm telling them how they should have lived, and how we all must live. But I hear a burbling and gurgling; I think the resident Lockean "experts" have something to say about "consent," and no doubt will explain this all to us, clearly and concisely:

> The literature on Locke's theory of consent tends to focus on how Locke does or does not successfully answer the following objection: few people have actually consented to their governments ...
>
> Simmons claims that Locke's arguments push toward "philosophical anarchism" ...
>
> Hannah Pitkin ... claims that the logic of Locke's argument makes consent far less important in practice ...
>
> John Dunn takes a still different approach. He claims that it is anachronistic to read into Locke a modern conception of what counts as "consent" ...
>
> Recent scholarship has continued to probe these issues. Davis closely examines Locke's terminology and argues ...
>
> Van der Vossen makes a related argument, claiming that the initial consent of property owners is not ...
>
> Hoff goes still further, arguing that we need not even think of specific acts of tacit consent ...
>
> The interpretive school influenced by Strauss emphasizes ...
>
> According to Grant, Locke thinks that our acts of consent can in fact extend to cases ...
>
> One part of this debate is captured by the debate between Seliger and Kendall, the former viewing Locke as a constitutionalist and the latter viewing him ...

Oh, lord, just put your foot on their heads and shove them back into the tar. "Consent" is what you consent to. "Consent" in the context of government does not, and never has, and never can, mean, automatically, "democracy"—and even in the most democratic democracy, some portion of the population is eternally disaffected with some portion of the *laws that are made and enforced* on them, to which they never agreed at all. And every single day, right in the United States, babies are born screaming and crying into this world, and into a system of government that they never once gave one single word or action of "consent" to.

So much for "consent."

The Miserable Uselessness of the Monstrous Fantasy-World "State of Nature"

If you're the kind of person who wants to terrify little kids, I guess it's pretty easy to tell them that there is a horrible monster in the closet, or in another dimension underneath the bed, and that if they dare drift off to sleep, the monster is going to suddenly appear and *get them!* I don't know how evil you'd have to be to stoop to such depths of depravity, but I think it can't be very many steps down from trying to terrify all of mankind with terrible tales of a horrific "state of nature" that we all came up from and will descend to again "if we don't watch out," where every man is out to murder and rob and destroy every other man. It's right in there with telling tales of ghastly, hideous, voracious sea monsters that will gobble up entire ships and crews, just to try to stop men from venturing on the seas.

The entire "state of nature" theory is 100-percent pure running-sewage fiction—and that's about the nicest thing that can be said about it. Whether you want to pin it on Locke, or on Hobbes, or want to try to trace it back further, it doesn't matter, because it's all completely false, completely fiction, completely absurd, completely asinine. And if that isn't enough, it's downright evil. Probably this "state of nature" cackling madness reached its tar-pit-bottom nadir in the 20th century with John Rawls and his "original position" experiment, infecting the world with the pus of so-called "social justice" that uniformly is antisocial injustice. In memory of Rawls, I'll paraphrase Mark Twain's sentiment about Jane Austen and her writing: It seems a great pity that they allowed him to die a natural death.

Belief in the "state of nature" phantasm sets up an utterly false and impossible dichotomy of real present-time life facing against something that doesn't exist: a phony, made-up, no-see-um (but surely terrible, doncha' know) "state of nature" lurking somewhere behind us, or in the bushes, or in the closet, or under the bed, or around the next election bend, ready to gobble us up if we drop our guard. It's just like the monster under the bed: there's really a bed, and there's really a room—*but there is no monster.*

And there is no terrifying "state of nature" where life is "solitary, poor, nasty, brutish, and short." That was Hobbes's bleak and nightmarish fantasy-world landscape of the "state of nature," with his model of governance supposedly being the only thing keeping it from consuming us all. Hobbes must have been a wretched human being who thought every other human being was a selfish and self-centered monster who was out, always, to do grievous harm to him and everyone else in the world. It is a tragic view of humanity.

Any honest scan of humankind finds that the vast majority of people do have a strong innate sense of **ETHICS**—as I carefully defined, separately from "morals," at the beginning of this chapter. The majority are not selfish, horrid, materialist creatures out only for themselves or dedicated to a life of crime. The majority are trying to make life livable, and are the ones on the backs of whom mankind has advanced in culture and civilization. Always, no matter what kind of "government" was in play, people have largely looked out for one another.

Charity and help for each other, freely given—not enforced by tax collectors, tyrants, and bureaucrats (but I repeat myself)—have been the lifeblood of societies, even with no "government" pointing guns at the heads of the people. If this were not the case, none of us would be here now. No communities or societies or civilizations ever would have formed at all. It is individual human beings doing good works in the love and service of others that has advanced us. When a government starts to *enforce* and *demand* that which is in the heart and spirit of its people to carry out on their own, without a gun to their heads, that government begins to destroy the very fabric of society and culture.

Only a relatively small percent of human beings are predisposed to doing harm to others through theft, violence, or chicanery. As merely an example, a 2010 study written for the Population Association of America's 2011 annual meeting, titled "Growth in the U.S. Ex-Felon and Ex-Prisoner Population, 1948 to 2010," gave figures indicating that only about 8.6 percent of the adult U.S. population had a felony conviction.

We are not going to go diving off into that other bottomless academic tar pit of statistical wallowing and manipulation, but even if U.S. statistics are not representative of the population of mankind worldwide, perfectly reasonable estimates put the percentage of humans predisposed to chronically causing trouble and harm to others at no more than about 20 percent. It's been postulated, also reasonably, that even those usually are under the influence of a much smaller percentage who are truly dedicated to evil. Anybody who believes that there is not true, relentless evil in some small percentage of mankind is living in a fairyland that is as dangerous as the Hobbes/ Locke "state of nature" fairyland. There has always been an element of evil and criminality *in every society of mankind that ever has existed, and no form of government ever has eliminated it or ever will.* All that governments of any description can do is contain the evil and the harmful, and sequester them from rational and civilized society. That will not change until mankind finds a way to make the insane sane, because all criminality is itself a form of insanity. The field of psychiatry won't do it because that field has attracted some of the 20 percent who are most evil.

But that leaves about *80 percent of the human race* who are decent, caring individuals who want to have a life of peace and security, and want the same for their fellow man.

It is only when the small percentage of truly evil people, or their influenced lackeys, get the reins of *the power to make and enforce laws* that anything resembling the nightmarish Hobbes/Locke "state of nature" condition arises, with horrors and bloodshed aplenty. We certainly have examples such as Hitler and Stalin to make that point inarguably. But that *does not mean* that all of mankind is evil. It is quite the contrary. The vast majority of mankind is basically good and seeking not only to survive, but to aid the survival of their fellow man, and of all of life.

Locke's fantasy-world "state of nature" was sheer unbridled anarchy amongst people who he claimed were all "equal and independent." In early letters, Locke mewled over fear of anarchy, but in truth he was a fanatical anarchist. Samuel Colt wasn't the cause of the Wild West; John Locke said that the "state of nature" was complete anarchistic vigilantism in which "equals" all had the right to summarily execute one another for any transgression without regard to its severity. Don't take my word for it. Here he is now, from *Two Essays on Government*:

> There being nothing more evident, than that creatures of the same species and rank, promiscuously born to all the same advantages of nature, and the use of the same faculties, should also be equal one amongst another without subordination or subjection ... if any one in the state of nature may punish another for any evil he has done, every one may do so: for in that state of perfect equality, where naturally there is no superiority or jurisdiction of one over another, what any may do in prosecution of that law, every one must needs have a right to do. ... Every man hath a right to punish the offender, and be executioner of the Law of Nature. ...
>
> Man being born, as has been proved, with a title to perfect freedom, and an uncontrouled enjoyment of all the rights and privileges of the law of nature, equally with any other man, or number of men in the world, hath by nature a power, not only to preserve his property, that is, his life, liberty and estate, against the injuries and attempts of other men; but to judge of, and punish the breaches of that law in others, as he is persuaded the offence deserves, even with death itself, in crimes where the heinousness of the fact, in his opinion, requires it.

And we're back on the Horror-Movie-Merry-Go-Round to Nowhere, where there is "survival of the equalist" among the *uberequal* man-animals, who are *uberequal* just like all the other beasts of the field, who—of course—are all entirely equal to each other within their own species, and are entirely "independent" of each other. (Stop laughing; this is The One True Gospel of Academia and its Overlords. You're not equal to them—even though they insist that we all are created equal. Understand?)

It isn't a question of whether Locke is mad; it's a question of how mad can a human being get and still be allowed to walk around among the rest of us. Apparently the answer is "John Locke."

If there ever had been any such "state of nature" among men, none of us would be here. There would be no civilization at all. There would be no community at all. There would be no government at all. There would be no religion at all. There would be no human race.

These insane theories of Locke became the fuse and the explosives that set off the bloodiest revolutions in history.

"A Title to Perfect Freedom"

Yet another frothing poison erupting from Locke's diseased mind is "perfect freedom." Freedom from what? Freedom to what? Are we free of gravity? Are we free of a need for food and water? Are we free of a need for companionship? Are we free of a need to procreate? Are we free from the elements of storms and searing heat and freezing cold? Are we free from the threats of the encroaching chaos of uncontrolled natural environments, plant and animal? Are we free from the thoughts and needs and wants and suffering of others? That's back to Locke's nuttiness of all being "independent," and his loopy proclamation of "perfect equality," and it's all chatteringly absurd. Reading Locke is reading fantasy fiction, not philosophy—and even as fiction, it's really, really bad fiction.

There is no "perfect freedom" for any human being to have any "title" to, nor any such "perfect equality," and the sooner such toxic cancerous ideas can be evacuated from mankind and his governments, the sooner we all can start to heal and recover from the harm done by these group hallucinations and psychoses. We all are in this together. There are no such "absolutes" as Locke dreamed up in his nightmarescape world. They are wicked fiction.

Without boundaries and barriers and rules, whether those are self-imposed or imposed by the physical universe in nature, or by a sovereign, or by a Congress, or by God, or by the scout leader, the word and the concept of "freedom" would be an empty infinite vacuum completely devoid of meaning. The frantic quest for absolute "freedom" is itself a miserable madness.

Reasonable freedoms are of course desirable, of course needed for human happiness and fulfillment and accomplishment. But it's also true that the entire human race managed somehow to limp along for thousands of years before John Locke came along to preach at us all about "perfect equality" and "independence" and "natural rights" and "perfect freedom," all of it out of his feverish fantasies about a world that never has existed and never can exist.

His madness showed up, for example, in the frothingly murderous shouts of "Liberté, égalité, fraternité!" in the French revolution and the

Reign of Terror. Then as many as a million people were slaughtered. France adopted it as it motto. France, as I write, has been invaded by immigration, its rich history and culture being eroded away daily, and its people being attacked and slaughtered in the streets, all in the name of "Liberty, equality, fraternity!" It is cultural suicide.

Locke's "State of Nature" Supposedly is Right Now, All Around You
John Locke must have woken up one day and, sitting up with a sudden chill of momentary sanity, realized how patently nuts his "state of nature" dogma was (which he essentially had stolen from Hobbes), so he dashed off an attempt at justifying it:

> It is often asked as a mighty objection, where are, or ever were there any men in such a state of nature? To which it may suffice as an answer at present, that since all princes and rulers of independent governments all through the world, are in a state of nature, it is plain the world never was, nor ever will be, without numbers of men in that state.

By the time he got to his feather pen, the fever must have been back on him, because the "explanation" is even nuttier than the original fantastic "state of nature" fiction.

But, of course, it's Locke, so Locke's twin self-canceling mandates of "equal" and "independent" have to extend not only to "all men," but to all the *nations* of man, so of course that means that every nation is "equal" and "independent"—which on its face is garbage a cat wouldn't drag away. Every nation is uniquely different: different in natural resources, different in industry, different in population, different in culture, different in art, different in music, different in ambitions, different in geography, different in every conceivable detail, while pompous and degreed buffoons sit in state departments attempting to shove a loaf of Lockean "equality" down each other's throats—as though it would even mean anything if they could.

No nation is independent. Every nation is interdependent!

Any nation or national leader that presumes itself "equal and independent" to all other nations, and presumes itself in anything resembling the "state of nature" of either Hobbes or Locke, will be in an eternal state of war, which never otherwise can lead to anything but chaos, death, and destruction.

Nations all share this same planet, and so all are interdependent, and their only mission in relation to any other nation should be a harmonious co-existence that is mutually beneficial. No human being can live any kind of livable life in a constant rigid state of "fight or flight," and as the macrocosm reflects the microcosm, no nation can long endure that considers itself surrounded always by mortal enemies, living always in terror or antagonism.

For mankind to progress toward peace and sanity in its governance, it must come to recognize sovereignty not as a license to attack and harm its neighbors, but as the ultimate responsibility and duty of helping its neighbors achieve peace, prosperity, and security for themselves.

The Chalice of Poison

No poisoner ever handed any intended victim a chalice of pure poison. For any poison to be effective, the intended victim has to believe that it is something desirable or healthy or appealing. So it is with the poison of John Locke. Of course there are truths in Locke's works that disguise the poisonous fallacies. If there weren't, they never would have been swallowed.

The body of an intended poisoning victim attempts to process and assimilate the food or drink carrying the poison, and it is that pro-survival attempt of the body's system to process and assimilate the good that introduces the poison into the system and weakens it, and possibly kills it.

So it is with the body politic's attempts to process and assimilate the sensible concepts that Locke stole from such philosophical giants such as Aristotle and Aquinas, but then stirred into his own bubbling cauldron of toxic philosophic sophistry, fatally laced with contradictory and fatuously false fiction.

The United States of America, as great as it is—and that is not lip service; it is a great nation of wonderful, caring people—was given a false goal as a drop of deadly poison in the ambrosia of its founding ideals: The poison is "equality."

Ever since, it has been endlessly engaged in shoving "equality" at its citizens, when its citizens are not even slightly "equal" to each other. No amount of legislation ever is going to make everyone "equal," and all legislation aimed at that false goal is fatally flawed.

The U.S. also is constantly engaged in exporting Lockean "created equal" lunacy and all its trappings, exporting it with smart bombs if necessary. Meanwhile, the U.S. itself, which sold and continues to sell the world this Lockean bill of goods as the "land of the free" and the shining model of "government by consent of the governed," is among the most super-controlled, hyper-policed nation in history. Far beyond its uniformed armed forces, police forces, border forces, drug forces, and security forces making air travel a living hell, it has entire standing armies in business suits, from federal level down to township, running ragged to enforce its countless regulations and crushing taxes and licensing fees and codes. And it will keep right on dropping leaflets and smart bombs, indiscriminately, on anybody who isn't shaping up quick enough to join the ranks of the "equal."

It first tells everyone in the world, individual and nation alike, that they are all "equal" and "free," creating a flock of nothing but shepherds, then issues code after code, law after law, regulation after regulation, tax after tax, fee after fee, bomb after bomb, to cattle-prod the flock of shepherds toward greater "equality."

This is the Lockean legacy. This is the Lockean lunacy. This is the realization of Locke's own barking mad assertion that "most men have some madness in them," because attempting to live in the Fool's Paradise he created will drive any man to madness.

The Simple Reality of Governance

About the most concise and generalized summation of the governance of man in civic, cultural, and national groups, pre-Locke, is that he uniformly has been governed by the most unequal among him.

Whether through conquest by a superior force of arms or thought, or through succession of a genetic line that by some device had gained power and authority, or through trust in religious leadership, or through assumed divine right, or through tribal leadership determined by a thousand different competitive criteria, or through some conglomerated combination of the above, man marched forward for centuries under the order and rule of governance by leaders who were viewed as decidedly *unequal,* and whose seat of power and authority was easily located. Some have been benign and successful leaders loved by their people, some have been bloodthirsty and psychotic tyrants, many have been middling. (Down South, "middling" is a grade of cotton.)

Whether a leader is good, bad, or mediocre, a subject or citizen could point to one or a small handful of the markedly unequal and say (or whisper), "There's the boss." Even the manageably small Greek city-states were ruled by succession. Their attempt in Athens at a form of democracy introduced the idea of the governed having a say in their government—not that it ultimately was a roaring success. As Thucydides said about democracy under Pericles, "It was in theory a democracy, but in fact it became the rule of the first Athenian"— meaning Pericles as "first" in leadership.

Well, there's nothing inherently wrong with a "first Athenian" or a "first" in any form or type of government, as long as the leader is an effective leader whose first interest is the wellbeing of those he represents and leads. But the idea of some form of government where everybody is "equal" is pure Lockean lunacy. Simply ejecting that madness from the United States government, or any government anywhere, could effect a renewal of all the wonderful goals and purposes of its founding, a resurgence, a renaissance in human relations that could out-renaissance the Renaissance, and could be a true age of Enlightenment, absent the tar of "equality."

All effective and successful governance, and business, for that matter, in all the long history of mankind has been based on some form hierarchy. Somebody has to be in charge of things taking responsibility for the whole show, and no such leader can be successful at anything for long without a hierarchical support staff on a sensible form of organization that allows for a chain of command and the easy exchange of relevant communication.

Regardless of whether a form of government is a monarchy or a republic or a democracy, all government fails to the exact degree that it forgets its only purpose: it must be working for the good of the people that its serves, and it must serve the needs of the people within its realm and jurisdiction.

9. How Rights Go Wrong: Tolerating the Intolerable
The Hopelessness of Homogenizing Human Beings

According to philosopher Alasdair MacIntyre, in his book *Whose Justice? Which Rationality?*:

> There is no expression in any ancient or medieval language correctly translated by our expression "a right" until near the close of the middle ages: the concept lacks any means of expression in Hebrew, Greek, Latin, or Arabic, classical or medieval, before about 1400, let alone in Old English, or in Japanese even as late as the mid-nineteenth century.

But we just learned in the previous chapter, from the ever-so-prestigious Stanford University, that "the **most central concept** in Locke's **political philosophy** is his **theory of natural law** and *natural rights.*" Apparently, none of these alleged "rights" were "natural" enough for most human beings even to develop a word to describe them for thousands of years. So with that firmly in mind, held onto with a white-knuckled grip, let's take a close look at Locke's "rationale" for the mysterious existence of "natural rights" that there was no language to describe (stripped of about two gallons of tar, bold emphasis added):

> Man [is] born, as has been proved, with **a title to perfect freedom**, and an uncontrouled [sic] enjoyment of **all the rights** and privileges **of the law of nature, equally with any other man** ... The **law of nature [is] unwritten**, and so **no where [sic] to be found but in the minds of men.**

(Blink) What? That can't be right. These "natural rights" are *unwritten*? They are "*no where [sic] to be found but in the minds of men*"? You mean that whatever anybody "thinks" is a "right" suddenly becomes a "natural right"?

There are about 40 billion people around the world at any given moment typing or preaching or lecturing or legislating or yelling or protesting or rioting or shooting or bombing or whining about rights, rights, rights, rights, rights—their rights, other people's right, the rights of the downtrodden, the rights of this race or of that race, or of this religion or of that religion, or of this gender or of that gender or of no gender, or of some mode of sexual perversity, or of illegal invaders and squatters, or, or, or, or, or.

The so-called United Nations spends billions of dollars annually (of other people's money) on an endless crusade of rights, rights, rights, rights, rights! They even wave around a *Universal Declaration of Human Rights* that goes on for *pages*, listing right after right after right that they claim everybody in the world is *entitled to*. And just as though that weren't enough, they've even got a United Nations Human Rights Council with *47 people on it* (all very learned "experts," I'm certain), and they've got a United Nations Human Rights Committee with "18 experts" on it. I'm sure all those experts must do something besides sight-see and take expensive lunches on expense accounts (using other people's money). And every last bit of this insistence on rights, rights, rights, rights, rights—All. Of. It.— comes *directly* from what you just read above by John Locke.

We've simply got to back up and try reading that again, maybe scraping away a little more of the tar that Locke smears all over everything. We've already, in the previous chapter, eradicated his nonsense about "perfect freedom," so we can scrape that away, and maybe a little more of the junk, and get down to his oh-so-important "central concept" of "natural rights" that supposedly come to us from "natural law." Let's try again:

> Man [is] born ... with **a title to ... all the rights** ... **of the law of nature** ... .
> The **law of nature [is] unwritten**, and so **no where to be found but in the minds of men**.

(Blink) What? That's *it*? That's the *total "foundation"* of all the alleged "rights" that half the world is screaming about and running around demanding, because they have a "title" to those "rights" granted by John Locke?

Well, at least we've certainly nailed down where this bizarre idea of "entitlement" comes from. That's its source, right there: "with a **title to**." Who handed down these "entitlements" from on high to all the people in the world running around screaming how "entitled" they are to rights, rights, rights, rights, rights? At this point, you're likely getting a creeping, chilling feeling about who the "Maker" or "Creator" might be who supposedly distributed all these "titles" of ownership of "rights" to all mankind. If you haven't guessed yet, are you sitting down?

It's no god at all, just a puny little 17th-century asthmatically fey, affected, effeminate, and feeble "philosopher" named John Locke.

If you feel like you've just been sucked through an air lock and are falling through endless space, take a moment to look around at the walls or your cat, or to really feel the chair you're sitting in, or to really *feel* anything you're touching or can reach out and touch, and the world should begin to right itself soon.

When the room stops spinning, there's a great peace to be found in coming to understand fully that much of humanity, for hundreds of years, has been living under the hallucinations and delusions of a very sick man named John Locke—and have believed it was the universe of their own God. It's like waking out of a grotesque, freakish, never-ending nightmare.

The problem, though, is the percentage of humanity still under the thrall of this Lockean madness, and the almost inconceivable toll in human life and human suffering that has resulted from it. That is a horror holocaust that is still taking place right this minute.

"Equality" and the "Equal Rights Under the Law" Fraud

Lockean louts will bleat and froth that the only thing the "equality" doctrine means, or ever meant, is that all people should have *equal access to* and *equal protection* under the *law*. Of course that's nonsense, because Locke said explicitly, expressly, even in very unLockean clarity, that mankind was all "equal and independent" in a "state of nature"—which, by Locke's own dogma existed before there were any man-made laws at all.

So under *what* law? Under *whose* law?

Is it "god's" law? Then which god? Islam's god, Allah, for example, proclaims that a woman is worth half as much as a man. That's inarguably written in black and white:

> "[Mohammed] said, 'Is not the evidence of two women equal to the witness of one man?' They replied in the affirmative. He said, 'This is the deficiency in her intelligence.'" —**Sahih Bukhari 6:301**

> "The male shall have the equal of the portion of two females" —**Quran 4:11**

That law? Well, there is certainly no "equality" there, is there? Islam also inarguably permits and condones slavery. *That* law? Or is it civil law under which we're all supposed to be "equal"? That could be troubling anywhere that Islam takes control, because Allah's laws *are* the civil laws within Islam, and no *civil laws* can be passed in an Islamic nation that in any way contradict the religious laws.

Law in England during the time of Locke, and law in the United States at the time of the *Declaration of Independence*—and indeed the law of most nations around the world at all relevant times leading up to the moment the slave trader Locke dreamed up the "created equal" dogma—entirely permitted and even expressly sanctioned some version of slavery or indentured servitude. Even right now, right this minute, as I sit and type this section of this manuscript, the Global Slavery Index—which anyone with the Internet can easily find—estimates that 45.8 million people "are in some form of modern slavery in 167 countries."

That law?

The *reductio ad absurdum* of that "reasoning" is that wherever slavery was or is countenanced *in the law*, it is perfectly fine for slaves to have equal access to and protection under *that civil law*, and therefore to have all the rights and freedoms *that are granted to slaves under that law.*

You, reader, being rational, can laugh at the babbling idiocy. I don't wish to "harsh your mellow," but as you laugh, try not to think this thought: Right now, in the world around you, the United Nations is foisting off on the world all the lunacy of Locke in its *Universal Declaration of Human Rights*, Article 1 of which begins just this way:

All human beings are born free and equal in dignity and rights.

As just one indication of how thoroughly brain-dead that statement is, the word "dignity," by dictionary definition, means:

Nobility or elevation of character; worthiness; dignity of sentiments; elevated rank, office, station, etc.; relative standing; rank. **—Random House Dictionary**

The quality or state of being worthy, honored, or esteemed; high rank, office, or position; a legal title of nobility or honor. **—Merriam-Webster Dictionary**

There are no words too strong to describe just how stupid the claim that all human beings are "equal in dignity" is—which of course entirely nullifies the very concept of "dignity." I believe the statement possibly qualifies as being more babblingly, bubblingly, maniacally insane than even John Locke managed to be.

And so with that "foundation," all the rest of this United Nations' *Universal Declaration of Human Rights*, along with all of John Locke's Mad Hatter tea cups, floats above a nonexistent floor suspended in tar. Do you feel the sucking undercurrents of the tar, as you ride round and round and round on another Lockean Merry-Go-Round of Madness, sinking, sinking, sinking into circularity?

It's with just that kind of circularity that the subject of human "rights"—which should be the most benign and beneficial ideological concept that could be applied to human interaction and to elevating the state of mankind's civilizations—has been usurped, stolen, by some of the most destructive and totalitarian groups and individuals on planet Earth, and has been turned into a weapon of mass destruction in an effort to either subjugate all of mankind, or to wipe it out of existence.

Not one word of the paragraph above is exaggeration or hyperbole. It may be understatement. Taking first the totalitarian desire to subjugate all mankind, it comes hidden in the Trojan Horse of the "right" of "religious freedom."

Political Totalitarianism Disguised in the Robes of "Religion"
Consulting again the "John Locke—Facts & Summary" page at History.com (and they should know, shouldn't they) reveals this pithy précis of Locke's "toleration," bold emphasis added:

> In three "Letters Concerning Toleration" (1689-92), Locke suggested that governments should respect freedom of religion **except when the dissenting belief was a threat to public order.** Atheists (whose oaths could not be trusted) and Catholics (who owed allegiance to an external ruler) were thus excluded from his scheme.

That bold phrase in the quote above is one thing that Locke got right—but it has been almost wholly ignored ever since by every idiot banging the drum for the unqualified "right" of "religious freedom." Now we're going to turn to more of Locke's own words on this subject, and in doing so are going to discover, step by step, just exactly how infamously ignorant the man was of perhaps the greatest threat to mankind and his civilizations that has ever existed:

> The public good is the rule and measure of all law-making. ...
> **If any thing pass in a religious meeting seditiously, and contrary to the public peace, it is to be punished** in the same manner, and no otherwise than as if it had happened in a fair or market. ...
> **No opinions contrary to human society, or to those moral rules which are necessary to the preservation of civil society, are to be tolerated by the magistrate [government].** But of those indeed examples in any church are rare. For **no sect can easily arrive to such a degree of madness, as that it should think fit to teach, for doctrines of religion, such things as manifestly undermine the foundations of society,** and are therefore condemned by the judgment of all mankind.

Locke's ignorance of Islam in that statement above is downright staggering. There's nothing wrong with ignorance, per se—unless you're too stupid to realize your own ignorance of a subject. Ignorance is not stupidity; ignorance is merely lacking in knowledge or information about a subject, and all of us are ignorant of many subjects we haven't pursued. Stupidity could well be defined as not realizing how ignorant you are, and not bothering to find out, or, worse, refusing to find out the relevant facts about something before mouthing off about it. In this arena, Locke was both ignorant and unforgivably stupid. Let's get the bare truth stated thoroughly, succinctly, and dispassionately, without bias or emotion, right at the outset, as will then be proven beyond any shade of doubt:

> *Islam is a totalitarian political nation-without-borders whose unquestionable, clearly stated goal is to overthrow all man-made nations on earth and replace them with a global theocracy known as a caliphate, and in doing so to eradicate all other religions and religious freedom. The fact that it has the metaphysical component of a self-proclaimed prophet who claimed to have spoken directly to an angel named Gabriel with messages to and from a god called Allah does not make it any less of a totalitarian political nation-without-borders whose expressly stated goal is to overthrow all man-made nations, and all other religions, and all rights to religious freedom on Earth.*

If you, like Locke, are ignorant of Islam, and if the only thing you know and believe about it is dishonest propaganda that Islam itself spreads through its own agents in governments and in the "mainstream" media, then the above incontrovertible facts may initially upset you or "trigger" you or hurt your feelings. If so, it's not my intention or purpose to do so, but it is my intention and purpose to tell the facts about the subject, even if they aren't pleasant, and I'm happy to share with you, below, information that has been willfully withheld from you by people who don't have your best interests at heart. But if you're ignorant of the facts, and *also* too stupid to get yourself adequately informed, then you'd do well to destroy this book and not read another word of it. If you go on with me from here, I'm about to prove what I just said above conclusively. If you go forward from this paragraph, there will be no going back. Your choice. Make it now.

To begin, this is an excerpt from a well-documented article by

Vijay Kumar, "The Muslim Mosque: A State Within a State":

> The Kaaba in Mecca was not built as an Islamic Mosque. It was an ancient temple that had been shared by polytheists, Christians, Jews, and Hindus, honoring 360 different deities. In 630 A.D. the Kaaba was captured by Islam in its military invasion and conquest of Mecca.
>
> On the day of its capture, Mohammed delivered an address at the Kaaba in military dress and helmet, according to Ayatullah Ja'far Subhani in his book, *The Message*:
>
>> "Bear in mind that every claim of privilege, whether that of blood or property is abolished ... I reject all claims relating to life and property and all imaginary honors of the past, and declare them to be baseless ... A Muslim is the brother of another Muslim and all the Muslims are brothers of one another and constitute one hand as against the non-Muslims. The blood of every one of them is equal to that of others and even the smallest among them can make a promise on behalf of others." **—Mohammed**

According to Islam's own *officially approved biography* of Mohammed (or Muhammad, or however you elect to spell the man's name), he built an army as a robber baron attacking the rich caravans crossing the deserts from the East, and dividing the "booty" with his men—who all had to bow down to him as the self-proclaimed "prophet" of the new "religion" he had created. Mohammed had grown up in Mecca, but he began having "visions" and hearing voices, and behaving so peculiarly that he ultimately was forced to flee because of it.

In much the same way as he robbed the caravans, he took most of his new "religion" from the long-existing Judeo-Christian teachings—down to and including its god, Yahweh, who Mohammed renamed "Allah." He also took from that religion the angel Gabriel, who Mohammed claimed came in private visits to him in a cave to deliver this new religion. He took Adam and Eve from the Judeo-Christian teachings, and even Jesus and Mary, redefining them in vastly different roles that fit his new religion. Not settling for that, he even took the very founder of the Judeo-Christian religions, Abraham, who Mohammed claimed had built the Kaaba (or Ka'bah, or however you choose to spell it) for the later benefit of Mohammed and his crew. Mohammed insisted that Adam first built it, then it was destroyed, then Abraham came along and rebuilt it, knowing, somehow, that Mohammed would come along later to own it.

So once Mohammed got a big enough army, he came back to Mecca, lied to the city fathers to get inside the gates, and exacted his revenge by personally destroying all the religious artifacts and idols of the Christians, Jews, and polytheists in the Kaaba. That's when he made his militant and political speech quoted above.

If you think that one word of the above is incorrect, then you don't know Islam and its history, or the "official" biography of Mohammed. It's all there, but it isn't all going to be reprinted here. It's easily available if you want to "fact-check" this.

First and foremost, after being a robber baron, Mohammed was a *political dictator and military conqueror*, who declared absolutely and unequivocally, once his invading army had conquered Mecca, that Islam was *a military and political state without borders*; that *all Muslims anywhere in the world* were united as *"one hand against the non-Muslims;"* and that the enemies of Islam until the end of time would be *all non-Muslims, and all non-Islamic nation-states.*

The very word "Islam" means, literally, *"submission."* The very word "Muslim" means literally *"one who submits."* This isn't accidental; Mohammed was a warlord who wanted all the world to submit and bow down before him and his dogma.

The documentation on all the above is so overwhelming—for anyone who will open his eyes and look—that it takes a truly dedicated idiot even to attempt to contradict it. Here is just some of it, quoted directly from Islam's own teachings and authorities:

The Believers are but a single brotherhood. —**Quran 49:10**

A Muslim has no nationality except his belief. —**Syed Qutb**

Islam wishes to destroy all states and governments anywhere on the face of the earth which are opposed to the ideology and program of Islam regardless of the country or the nation which rules it. The purpose of Islam is to set up a State on the basis of its own ideology and program. —**Syed Abul A'ala Maududi**

Islam does not recognize geographical boundaries, nor does it acknowledge racial and blood differences, considering all Muslims as one Umma [nation] ... Every inch of land inhabited by Muslims is their fatherland. —**Hasan al-**

Banna, founder of Muslim Brotherhood

All Muslims form a single nation. —**Constitution of the Islamic Republic of Iran**

The mosques are our barracks. And the believers our Army. —**Turkish Prime Minister Tayyip Erdogan**

When you are called (by the Muslim ruler [Imam]) for fighting, go forth immediately. —**Mohammed; Hadith, Bukhari 52:79; Narrated Ibn 'Abbas**

If the Imam calls a group of people to arms, they are obliged to join his military forces. —**Ibn Qudama, al-Mughni**

The Ikhwan [Muslim Brotherhood] must understand that their work in America is a kind of grand Jihad in eliminating and destroying the Western civilization from within and "sabotaging" its miserable house by their hands and the hands of the believers so that it is eliminated and [Allah's] religion is made victorious over all other religions. —**Muslim Brotherhood, "General Strategic Goal for the Group in North America"**

Act like you are his friend. Then kill him. —**Sheik Muburak Gilani, founder of Jamaat ul-Fuqra, explaining how to kill American infidels**

Allah is our objective; the Quran is our constitution, the Prophet is our leader; Jihad is our way; and death for the sake of Allah is the highest of our aspirations. —**Credo of the Muslim Brotherhood**

If anyone desires a religion other than Islam (submission to Allah), never will it be accepted of him. —**Quran 3:85**

Fight and slay the unbelievers wherever ye find them, and seize them, beleaguer them, and lie in wait for them in every stratagem (of war). —**Quran 9:5**

There is a clear indication of the obligation to fight the People of the Book [Christians and Jews], and of the fact that God doubles the reward of those who fight them. Jihad is not against polytheists alone, but against all who do not embrace Islam." —**Hasan al-Banna, founder of Muslim Brotherhood**

We shall put yokes on the necks of the Unbelievers. —**Quran 34:33**

How blind or insane—or liberal, or conservative—do you have to be that you cannot see a deadly enemy, completely dedicated to your submission or death, staring you right in the face and telling you in the plainest possible language that he is going to dominate you and all of your nation, or is going to annihilate you? (Not literally "you," dear reader; I know you're smarter than that, or you wouldn't still be reading.)

In light of the above, now read this chattering madness from Locke in his screed on "toleration":

> **That church can have no right to be tolerated by the magistrate [government]**, which is constituted upon such a bottom, that **all those who enter into it, do thereby *ipso facto* deliver themselves up to the protection and service of another prince.** For by this means the magistrate would give way to the settling of **a foreign jurisdiction in his own country**, and suffer **his own people to be listed,** as it were, for **soldiers against his own government.**

A more exact description of Islam could hardly be made. Every mosque in the world, in every nation in the world, is precisely a *foreign jurisdiction in that nation*, and every person who attends a mosque in a non-Muslim nation *becomes a soldier against his own government*, ordered unequivocally by Islam, as quoted earlier, to fight if ordered by the Imam. Yet Locke specifically mandates "toleration" for the "Mahometans," as he called Muslims.

It is inarguable that the Quran (or Koran, or Qu'ran, or however you want to spell it) is a *political document*. The Quran, along with the Sunnah—the habits and practices of Mohammed—*is the constitution* of the Kingdom of Saudi Arabia, which is the birthplace of Islam, and the Kaaba is, symbolically, the worldwide *political* seat of Islam. Every mosque in the world—which is a paramilitary and political outpost—has a visible indicator, the *mihrab*, that points toward the Kaaba, and all Muslims everywhere in the world must bow toward the Kaaba when in a mosque. That's because it is the seat of their worldwide political nation—whether any one of them knows it or not. A very high percentage of so-called "Muslims" can't read at all, and a higher percentage still cannot read Arabic, so the only thing they know about "Islam" is what they are told. Really, they are dilettantes, not true Muslims. The *real* Muslims, the ones who actually know and understand Islam, are invariably on a permanent *jihad* to overthrow all man-made nations and all other religions in the world, by any means. Period.

Islamic nations—the ones that already have been overwhelmed and overthrown by Islam in the past 1,400 years—have the Quran as an *integral part* of their *political constitutions,* and all Islamic nations forbid any civil law that goes counter to the Quran and Islam—and of course Islam includes Sharia law. Those nations include, e.g., Iran, Iraq, Pakistan, Afghanistan, Egypt, Syria, Libya, Palestine, Yemen, Algeria, Bahrain, Morocco, Somalia, and Malaysia.

Because Islam is a *totalitarian political theocracy,* Sharia law *is civic law*, in the fullest sense of the term, and wherever it takes the slightest toe-hold, it seeks to overthrow the man-made laws of that nation and supplant them with the Quran, the Sunnah, and Sharia law.

Any government on earth following the lunatic "toleration" mandates of John Locke, and thereby allowing Islam to plant its paramilitary outposts called "mosques" on its soil, is willfully exposing its citizens to an infiltration of an openly declared hostile force dedicated to the overthrow of that nation. Any government that would do that to its people is a government in treason to its citizens and to its mandate to protect their security. As things currently stand, that includes the United States.

The deadly poison in Locke's dogma on "toleration" is that while he happily excludes atheists and Catholics from his "tolerating" largesse, he welcomes Islam with open arms, demonstrating his profound ignorance of it with every new statement:

> **Nobody is born a member of any church**; otherwise the religion of parents would descend unto children by the same right of inheritance as their temporal estates, and everyone would hold his faith by the same tenure he does his lands, than which **nothing can be imagined more absurd**.

However "absurd" Locke thought that such an idea was, that's the exact measure of his embarrassing ignorance of Islam. The website *Islam Questions and Answers* says unequivocally: "The child who is born to two Muslim parents is ruled to be a Muslim, according to scholarly consensus. If the parents have different religions, then the child follows the one who is Muslim, whether it is the father or the mother." The website *Islamweb* puts it this way—and I wouldn't wish to change a syllable of it:

> The majority of Muslim scholars (Hanafis, Shaafi'is and Hanbalis) maintained that the key factor in this regard is that either parent is Muslim, be it the mother or father; the children are then Muslims as a consequence of their Muslim parent, because Islam prevails and no other religion prevails over it, since it is the religion of Allah which He is pleased with for His slaves.

John Locke goes on in his blithering, blathering sermon on "toleration":

> Another more **secret evil, but more dangerous to the commonwealth [government]**, is when **men arrogate to themselves, and to those of their own sect, some peculiar prerogative covered over with a specious show of deceitful words**, but in effect **opposite to the civil rights of the community**. For example: We cannot find any sect that teaches expressly and openly, that men are not obliged to keep their promise.

There, Locke all but brags about his ignorance of the Islamic doctrine of *taqiyya*: Lying to "infidels"—nonbelievers—is wholly acceptable in Islam as long as it forwards the cause of Islam. Mohammed famously said, "War is deceit," and Mohammed is proclaimed to be the "perfect model" for all Muslims to follow. Oh, but Locke is by no means done dictating to everyone in the world what they need to "tolerate":

> **No man by nature is bound unto any particular church or sect**, but everyone joins himself voluntarily to that society in which he believes he has found that profession and worship which is truly acceptable to God. The hope of salvation, as it was the only cause of his entrance into that communion, so it can be the only reason of his stay there. For **if afterwards he discover anything either erroneous in the doctrine or incongruous in the worship of that society** to which he has joined himself, **why should it not be as free for him to go out as it was to enter**?

There's Locke making a non-point with his endless flood of useless rhetorical questions. Well, of course it "should" be "free for him to go out"—in the case of an actual *religion*, rather than a political totalitarianism—but here we are discussing *Islam*, and there is *no exit from Islam*. Apostasy is a death sentence:

> Whoever changed his Islamic religion, then kill him." **— Mohammed; Hadith, Bukhari 84:57; Narrated 'Ikrima**

For Locke, though, it was too much trouble, apparently, to bother finding out what he was talking about, so he just rambled on, and on, and on, setting up anyone who fell for his lunacy to be infiltrated and overwhelmed and even slaughtered:

> **These**, therefore, and the like, **who attribute unto the faithful, religious, and orthodox**, that is, in plain terms, **unto themselves, any peculiar privilege or power above other mortals, in civil concernments**; or who **upon pretence [sic] of religion** do **challenge any manner of authority over such as are not associated with them in their ecclesiastical communion**, I say these have **no right to be tolerated by the magistrate**; as neither **those that will not own and teach the duty of tolerating all men in matters of mere religion.** For what do all these and the like doctrines signify, but that **they may and are ready upon any occasion to seize the Government and possess themselves of the estates and fortunes of their fellow subjects**; and that **they only ask leave to be tolerated by the magistrate so long until they find themselves strong enough to effect it?**

John Locke just described Islam *precisely* with his rhetorical questions—oblivious throughout that he was describing Islam. For over 14 centuries Islam's *primary weapon* against nation-states and civilizations and other religions has been infiltration and invasion by immigration, knowingly, willfully using the religious tolerance of the hosting nations to slowly take over, overthrow, and destroy the host nation and its culture. I'm going to quote here another passage by Vijay Kumar that is eloquently germane, this taken from his seminal tract called "Islam and the Divine Deception":

> There are parasitic plants, such as the Virginia Creeper and the Strangler Fig, that start out as almost imperceptible growths on their host plants or trees. They send their tendrils down into the soil to suck out the nutrients, and even tap into the very roots of the host. From their hosts, they derive protection and strength, as they grow rapidly to wrap their vines around the body of the host, and interleave their foliage with it in mockery of it. Eventually, they can choke the life out of the host. Where a Strangler Fig prevails, the tree inside it dies and rots, leaving the twisted, entangled vines of the living Strangler Fig standing alone as a new "tree."
>
> Such parasites never assimilate into the host; they stand apart, clinging to it, feeding off of it, taking its protection and nutrients—and smother the life out of it.
>
> Islam never assimilates, either. It stands apart in a non-Islamic civilization, clinging to it, enjoying and profiting from the freedoms, riches, pleasures, and rights of that society until it can overcome and dominate it,

no matter how long it takes, and supplant it with Islamic totalitarianism.

And that, precisely, is Islam and its divine deception: a covert paramilitary force that uniformly, for 1,400 years, has invaded nation after peaceful nation, often approaching not in war wear but in the robes of being a "religion," willfully deceiving the kind and decent people who have reached out to welcome and succor it, the hosts then only to be betrayed, slaughtered, overwhelmed, and overthrown without mercy, their temples and their art and their civilization destroyed in exact compliance with the "prophet" that taught the marauding invaders to call their mission of war a "religion of peace" to better deceive the infidels.

John Locke was a blithering idiot who was so ignorant of Islam that he described it perfectly as the one type of "religion" that could not possibly be tolerated by any government, while in the same document said emphatically that Muslims must be tolerated by all governments.

This is the utter madness guiding most of the world's governments and deliberative bodies today—including the United States and the United Nations, and courts around the world. Unless and until the remaining non-Islamic nations in the world, and all international political bodies such as the United Nations, name and deal with Islam for exactly what it is—a political entity—those nations and political bodies are willfully in treason to their constituents and citizens, and are knowingly, willfully putting their constituents and citizens at a high state of risk, while compromising their own very existence as a nation or political entity. To embrace and treat Islam as a "religion" is demonstrably cultural and national suicide. That has been proven conclusively by nations around the world for over 1,400 years.

If civic and governmental leaders are traitorous to their citizens and people for "tolerating" Islamic political and paramilitary invasion, even worse are religious leaders outside of Islam who fall for the unctuous lies of Islamic propaganda, and attempt to "ally" their own religions and followers with Islam. They are leading their lambs to slaughter, and betraying every principle of their own faith that they pretend to stand for.

A Buddhist spiritual leader named Ashin Wirathu has issued an observation to the world that rings with thousands of years of Buddhist wisdom, in a region of the world that Islam has already infiltrated to a dangerous degree: "You can be full of kindness and love, but you cannot sleep next to a mad dog. If we are weak, our land will become Muslim." Countless millions of people in the last 1,400 years have learned that lesson too late.

Whoever or whatever the people who identify themselves with the polity called Islam want to worship or pray to is of course entirely up to them. They do not, though, have any "right" to invade other peoples and nations and force their brand of totalitarian politicized dogma on those peoples and nations—no matter how much the delusions and hallucinations of either John Locke or Mohammed insist that they can.

While Islam is relentless in its traitorous deceit, using the "right" of religious freedom to carry out its goal to dominate and subjugate all of mankind to its totalitarian dogma, another group has similarly used traitorous deceit in abusing "rights" for an even more evil goal: the annihilation and eradication of mankind.

10. How Rights Go Wrong: Gender Slouching Toward Equality
House Husbands and Women's Quest for Manhood

This isn't about whether women should have the right to fight in battle or run a government or corporation, or whether men should have the right to wear frilly bras to sports bars, so if you're looking for a way to get your blood pressure pumped on that basis, you might want to skip this chapter. This is about insanely destructive goals and purposes versus rational constructive goals and purposes.

If you are reading this, and honestly are unable to find a *host* of differences between men and women, or if you believe that gender is some airy-fairy mental "spectrum," please stop reading this right now. Seriously. Please go away. Your staying will waste your time and mine. Even my dogs clearly understand that there are two genders—male and female—so if you can't understand this obvious and inarguable fact, you certainly won't be able to understand a word I'm saying. Give this book to someone who hasn't been brainwashed into vegetable status by the "experts" of academia and the psychoestablishment, and so is still able to think rationally. 'Bye. *Ciao. Au revoir. Auf Wiedersehen. Arrivederci. Sayonara. Adios.*

For those remaining: To the degree that any frantic quest in the modern world for gender "equality" is an effort to satisfy the most famous hallucination of the Golem of Philosophy, John Locke, expressed by Thomas Jefferson in the phrase "all men [*OMG! He must have meant 'persons'!*] are created equal," it's a pointless quest, a fool's errand. It makes the Holy Grail look like something you could pick up at any convenience store. It makes tilting at windmills seem sane.

The *reductio ad absurdum* of a quest for "gender equality" is "neuter"—also called in some sciences "rock." There are surgical procedures available to everyone who is on that quest. If you are on such a quest for "gender equality," I can't imagine why you're still here reading this, and didn't take advantage of the polite invitation in the second paragraph above for you to leave. If you were just gathering your bag and things, I would like to mention that availing yourself of those procedures will do a great service for natural selection, so I salute you. (Any materialists solved The Materialists' Conundrums yet? This might be a good test series for "survival of the equalest." At least the control group likely would have fun.)

Glorification of Sexual Perversion is War Against Mankind

The traditional family is the core of human existence. Heterosexual relationships and marriages came into existence as the guarantee for the future of mankind. The *purpose* of sex is procreation, and only heterosexual sex results in procreation. The *purpose* of sex is *not* transitory "pleasure;" sex is pleasurable so that its *purpose*—which is continuation of the race—will take place and mankind can go forward into the future.

Obsessive or fixated focus on sexual "pleasures" that are not heterosexual, practiced to the *exclusion* of heterosexual activities, are perversions. If you're offended by the word "perversion," you're welcome to stop reading, clutch your pearls, and leave through the same exit door as those who left at the second paragraph of this chapter, but it's a perfectly correct word in the English language that effectively describes the condition, "perversion" being defined as "any of various means of obtaining sexual gratification that are generally regarded as being abnormal." The word "abnormal" means "not normal, average, typical, or usual; deviating from a standard."

Every valid source of statistics available unequivocally reflects such sexual behavior as being *abnormal*, by definition. In January 2017, a Gallup poll reported that the total percentage of the U.S.

population who said they were lesbian, "gay," bisexual, or transgender was only 4.1 percent. By simple math, that means that 95.9 percent of the population is *not* homosexual, bisexual, or transgender. Those conditions—by statistics, simple math, and fundamental dictionary definitions—are *perversions*, and that's how I'm appropriately going to refer to them.

Efforts to debase, degrade, demean, ridicule, or compromise traditional heterosexual marriage and traditional families are efforts to destroy the future of the human race. Attacks on heterosexuality are attacks on the human race. Efforts to "train" or indoctrinate children in the "acceptability" of sexual perversions, or into the "acceptability" of surgically mutilating their genitals and reproductive organs, are efforts to eradicate the human race.

That is as obvious as daylight. It is so obvious and simple that it seems that any addlepated imbecilic dimwitted blockheaded mouth-breathing knuckle-dragging moron could figure it out. That may fully explain why academic "experts" and psychiatrists and styling-salon-coiffed TV personalities can't figure it out. This has nothing to do with any political party or any given religion; it has to do with sanity, intelligence, and *ethics* in a person that exceeds that person's immediate genital area or next frantic sexual romp.

Dedicated homosexuals are people with sexual perversions. There is nothing "glamorous" or "hip" about being a homosexual who is incapable of having a heterosexual relationship and procreating for the future of the human race. It is a rather pathetic disability worthy of empathy, not hatred or disgust. Being "gay" has become glorified in the culture in recent decades only because "gays" have leveraged the Lockean lunacy of "Oh, we're all eeeeeeeequal to you," and have thereby gotten into positions of power in politics and entertainment, and have thereby flooded the culture with propaganda campaigns whose only actual purpose is to destroy mankind.

The flood of propaganda for perversion has gotten so ridiculous that it's become practically impossible to find any entertainment or "news" media that isn't loaded and overloaded with glorification of being "gay" or some other brand of perversion. As an example, it seems that there's not a stand-up comedian standing any more who can make it through an hour show without getting in at least one withering diatribe of infantile school-yard name-calling against people who supposedly are mentally ill with the dreaded condition of "homophobia"—which, like all Lockean lunacy, doesn't exist. (None of these idiots are bright enough to figure out that "homo-" as a combining form means "same." Of course "phobia" means an "irrational fear," so in their juvenile bullying name-calling, they are accusing their targets of being "irrationally afraid of people who are the same as you." For heterosexuals, being "homophobic" would mean they have an irrational fear of other heterosexuals. Yes, it's all *just that idiotic.*)

As another example, count sometime the percentage of commentators and hosts on the "major" 24-hour "news" services and on TV networks that are homosexual (as of 2017), then compare those percentages to the actual percentage in the population. If you don't think that is a planned, strategized, organized, and orchestrated propaganda agenda, you may qualify for the "rock" gender status— and a mental status to match.

As for "gay rights," which really means "pervert rights," there's no rational reason at all that any dedicated homosexuals should have all the societal rights and benefits of heterosexual marriage and the *families* who are working responsibly to keep the human race going forward into the future, taking on all the responsibilities and costs of raising children, when the perverts are doing nothing whatsoever to uphold their responsibility to that *purpose*, and in fact are doing everything they can to debase, degrade, demean, ridicule, or compromise traditional heterosexual marriage and traditional families. The "trendy" pose of homosexual "couples" adopting children created by heterosexuals is really just a showy way to debase, degrade, demean, ridicule, or compromise traditional heterosexual marriage and traditional families.

I don't care, and neither should anybody care, if someone wants to have sex only with rutabagas. That is a "right" they certainly have, and are welcome to, as long as they do it in private and I don't have to be lectured endlessly about "rutabagaphobia"—through media *licensed by a government that is supported by taxes*—or have to deal with traffic tied up *by a local government using taxes* because of a "Rutabaga Partner Pride" parade.

Personally, I think it's a very sad state of affairs when a group of people's lives are so hollow, so empty, so meaningless, so purposeless that the only thing they can think of worth having a parade about is what they do for sex. But that's just my opinion. What's factual is that MentalHelp.net reports the following:

> According to the National Alliance on Mental Illness, the risk of a mental health condition, like depression, anxiety disorders, or post-traumatic stress disorder, is almost three times as high for youth and adults who identify as lesbian, gay, bisexual, or transgender (LGBT)—or those with a sexuality that doesn't apply to any existing category.

The National Alliance on Mental Health, in an article titled simply "LGBTQ," reports:

> LGBTQ individuals are almost 3 times more likely than others to experience a mental health condition such as major depression or generalized anxiety disorder. ...
> LGBTQ youth are 4 times more likely and questioning youth are 3 times more likely to attempt suicide, experience suicidal thoughts or engage in self-harm than straight people. Between 38-65% of transgender individuals experience suicidal ideation. ...
> The LGBTQ community reports higher rates of drug, alcohol and tobacco use than that of straight people. ... An estimated 20-30% of LGBTQ people abuse substances, compared to about 9% of the general population. 25% of LGBT people abuse alcohol, compared to 5-10% of the general population.

Many of the statistics on promiscuity and disease among the "LGBTQ" communities are equally grim, but they can easily be found online, so don't need to be trotted out here. It is poignant and moving that fellow human beings are experiencing these kinds of anguishes in life, for any reason. They need care and help, not hatred or abuse.

But it's also true that all such aberration is as *contagious as plague*, which is clearly reflected in the increasing percentages of such perversions among the population since the entertainment and information industries have begun flooding the culture with "glorification" of perversion. And it's also true that this statistically tiny portion of the population wreaks statistical hell on the culture in the spread of disease and drugs, legal and illegal. Even the Centers for Disease Control—who cheerfully use taxpayer dollars to promote perversion—confessed that as of 2010 (the last statistics they had available at the time of publication), men who had sex with men were responsible for 63 percent of the new HIV infections.

Any government or business that would put or allow such perversions into positions of sweeping power and influence is a government or business with a death wish, not just for itself, but for mankind. Any school or education system that would allow these kinds of perverted influences to be put into a classroom of children under any pretext has declared war on the next generation of the human race, and is a system that should be shuttered without waiting for the next dawn.

The Toxic Masculinity of Feminists

Women are the very definition of grace: "elegance or beauty of form, manner, motion, or action." That's not a comment on some false and phony "standard" of physical form or stature; that's a comment on the uncountable and immeasurable number of arts and graces, great and small, that women throughout the ages have infused into a family, into a home, into life itself.

It is an irony that only ever could have arisen out of such a tar pit of insanity as the Lockean lunacy of "equality" that the very word for describing such amazing grace—*feminine*—has been usurped and vandalized and weaponized by perverted females who are trying to be men (some of them doing an almost convincing job at their fraud), and by perverted males trying to be women (none of them even coming close), both sets of perverts, male and female, trying to turn women into men, while also doing all they can to turn men into women.

This entire "movement" comes not from rational human beings trying to elevate and glorify the status of either men or women. It comes from the tarry propaganda of perverts and "experts" in the psychoestablishment, and in academia, and in government, and in the media who are, themselves, mentally, spiritually, morally, and ethically deranged. Such perverts are at war with the human race, and use every dirty trick and dirty politician (but I repeat myself) at their disposal to stir up warfare against rational and ethical real women and real men.

It is war on the family, it is war on the future, it is war on children, it is war on procreation, it is war on women, and it is war on the human race. It is war.

It is a tiny, sick, perverted percentage of the population—but then, John Locke was among them. And he's the one who told them all that they are "equal." He was a physically and mentally and spiritually ill pervert, and his insane dogma is perverting the world.

Unperverting The Pitiful Tar-Pit Perversion of Philosophy

The first soul-searching anyone should engage in who is concerned with the issue of gender and sexuality is: do you actually have a gender-related problem, personally, that needs address (not "a dress"), or are you caught up in the group stampede to chase John Locke's tail on the merry-go-round to nowhere called "Equality"?

If there actually is a real-world situation personally affecting you, the next problem to solve—and probably the biggest one—is the right authorities to appeal to. Look not toward Washington, D.C., or your own governmental capital. They are not the creators of the gender roles and conditions, so they have *no effective authority or power* to change whatever needs changing, *and never will.* Yelling at the doctor to fix the leaky sink makes for soggy floors and frayed doctor nerves. The best that waving a pointed heel or lacy man-bra in the face of a lobbyist or congress... person ... . Waving it in the face of a government Representative or Senator can only produce *enforcement* at best, not societal acceptance and change. Even a moment of rational reflection confirms it. (If you're still reading this, I'm extending to you a presumption of capability of rational reflection.)

It isn't a political issue; it's a deeply ingrained spiritual, moral, ethical, and mental issue. The legislation and enforcement of a new law doesn't change the ancient religious codes, moral codes, ***ETHICAL***

CODES, and mandates, East and West, governing the deeply held beliefs and attitudes of the billions of people who subscribe to such codes governing sexual conduct—but more importantly it can never, ever change the inherent **ETHICS** and **SANITY** of those who are *sane* enough to know that only traditional roles of male and female, in heterosexual relationships, can keep the human race going into the future.

Do you want to help the survival of the human race, or do you want to harm it?

No matter how feverishly John Locke hallucinated the existence of a governmental body that in actual practice could operate superior to mankind's faiths, religions, and innate **ETHICS**, it has not come to pass in all the centuries since his loony decree that it should.

That is why all the demonstrations, riots, propaganda, and ass-strutting being done for "gay rights" and "gender equality" are nothing whatsoever but chaos theatre, designed not to bring about a better culture or society for mankind, but to disrupt and destroy it as much as possible.

The materialist and the atheist have no concerns for, and often even hold in contempt, the spiritual and **ETHICAL** underpinnings of gender relationships within any culture or society, and cry "Down with the differences, equality now!" Yeah, sure. Whatever. That's the war cry of warfare against mankind and the fomenting of chaos.

Some form of mutiny was pretty much the cowardly slinking dandy John Locke's solution to everything—as long as he could be somewhere else when it happened.

Of course Locke was a confirmed bachelor who is never known to have had any close personal relationship with a woman at all, which made the "great philosopher," naturally, the final "expert" on the subject of man-woman relationships and roles. So we probably ought to give him credit for establishing the modern standards for an "expert," as well.

There are lots of tails to chase on the endless merry-go-round-to-nowhere of Lockean lunacy—if you like that sort of view. So do you want to help the survival of the human race, or do you want to harm it?

11. How Rights Go Wrong: The Race Race
Circular Track, No Finish Line

On 18 July 1950—exactly one year, seven months, and eight days after issuing the *Universal Declaration of Human Rights* with its Lockean hallucination that "All human beings are born free and equal in dignity and rights"—the United Nations came up with a brilliant way of dismissing and demonizing any and all criticism concerning any issues related to race that might even *tend* to call its group-think delusion into question: It issued an imperialistic proclamation, called, informally, "The Race Question," that informed the world of this:

> For all practical social purposes "race" is not so much a biological phenomenon as a social myth.

If you go out into the world, and you think you see, with your own eyes, people who are of different races, you're the one who is nuts. The UN has proclaimed it. They not only proclaimed it, they proclaimed that "scientists have reached general agreements" to that effect, and further proclaimed that you better not *dare* question these "scientists":

> The competence and objectivity of the scientists who signed the document in its final form cannot be questioned.

So for 67 years, any scientist who has dared to submit scientific evidence to the contrary—and there's a mountain of it—has been condemned, branded, blackballed, smeared, and labeled as a heretic, a "racist," a "white supremacist," a "Nazi," a "fascist," or worse. Even mentioning this subject here is almost guaranteed to get me and this book condemned and vilified and smeared by some holier-than-thou virtue-signaling Social Justice Warrior as "racist"—and it will be someone who would happily get right in my face to demand, with spraying spittle, that while race is nothing but a myth, Black Lives Matter. The irony is always lost.

But facts are facts, and people who refuse to look at facts are the hateful bigots whose purpose is not to increase harmony and understanding between human beings—of any race—but to sow the exact kind of dissension and conflicts that their militant demands of forced "equality" inevitably create.

One of the most amusing ironies today is that the Holiest of Holies in the fanatical "everyone is equal" religion reside in the sanctum sanctorums of our colleges and universities, with Masters Degrees and PhDs—the "experts," doncha know—and right down the polished halls or across the quad from these "scientific" High Priests of Racial Equality an utterly *stupefying* program of *systemic institutional racism* is raging. They not only sit by and condone this madness, they buy expensive tickets and wave pom-poms and flags to promote it, and insist that their flock of indoctrinated students do the same.

The Systemic Institutional Racism of the NCAA, NBA, and NFL

A set of statistics was released recently, gathered from public information available on the Internet, that showed the following about three major universities:

University of Alabama

Percentage of student enrollment that is black: 10.7
Percentage of starting football team that is black: 91

Percentage of student enrollment that is white: 76.5
Percentage of starting football team that is white: 9

Clemson University
Percentage of student enrollment that is black: 6.6
Percentage of starting football team that is black: 78

Percentage of student enrollment that is white: 77.8
Percentage of starting football team that is white: 22

University of Southern California
Percentage of student enrollment that is black: 5.6
Percentage of starting football team that is black: 87

Percentage of student enrollment that is white: 60
Percentage of starting football team that is white: 12

That is simply *staggering* institutional racism *right inside* the very "scientific" universities that are preaching, teaching, lecturing, sermonizing, and issuing thundering proclamations that there are *no biological differences in races!* The reason that Asians aren't reflected in the statistics above is because they are so *racially* excluded in representation in NCAA football programs that it's statistically not worth mentioning. The hypocrisy defies all words.

If you think for a moment that I'm exaggerating this hideous systemic institutional racism, feel free to contact the universities yourself and demand some answers. We did. A researcher who helped compile data for this book sent emails to the presidents, and to the heads of the athletic departments, and where possible to a senior representative of the trustees of all three of the universities listed above, showing the statistical data above, and said the following (emails on file):

This seems inexplicable. My senior editor on this project has asked me to dig into it further, and I felt that due diligence required that I contact you first to get an official response and perspective on behalf of the administration, the trustees, and the athletics department.

I would be extremely grateful if each of you could comment, with any insights you might have into how this state of affairs came to be, and what, if anything, the university might do about it.

Those emails went to the following people:

University of Alabama
Dr. Stuart Bell, President; Matt Calderone, Deputy Secretary of the Board of Trustees; and Finus Gaston, Senior Associate Athletics Director.

Clemson University
Dr. James Clements, President; Angie Leidinger, Executive Secretary to the Board of Trustees and Vice President for External Affairs; and Michael Godfrey, Athletic Leadership Program.

University of Southern California
C. L. Max Nikias, President; Lynn Swann, Athletic Director

The last possible edit of this manuscript had to take place in late November 2017, and so far every person contacted ignored our requests for response. I urge you to contact them yourselves and attempt to get an answer to why they are practicing such blatant, obvious, inarguable racism in creating their football teams. Demand that all athletic teams in these tax-subsidized educational institutions reflect the racial percentages of the student body. See how far you get.

A similar situation of blatant systemic institutional racism is rampant in the NFL and the NBA. There's a downright amusing story from 1993, published by the Associated Press—"Survey Shows Lack of Jobs for Blacks"—in which Jesse Jackson Jr.'s Rainbow Commission for Fairness in Athletics was taking the National Basketball Association to task for the fact that 88 percent of the administrative jobs were held by white people. The word "irony" just gets wrung out after a while, but the irony was lost on Jackson and his group, and on the Associated Press, that in formulating the complaint, the Rainbow Commission for Fairness in Athletics stated that *78 percent of the players were black*. And it's about the same today. And that can be attributable to nothing whatsoever but systematic institutional racism in the selection of players: The NBA certifies every year that it considers black players better than white players by a factor of roughly 4 to 1.

At the time of publication of this book, the best statistics available show that the NFL regularly practices the same kind of in-your-face institutional racism, at only a slightly different rate. NFL starting players are about 70 percent black—even though blacks make up only about 13 percent of the U.S. population. The NFL and many of its teams get special tax breaks and subsidies, yet the U.S. government and many state governments continue to support this unconscionable extreme racism against whites, Asians, and other races in professional football.

None of this should be surprising about the NBA and the NFL, given that their recruitment pools are almost exclusively the colleges and universities, and given the inarguable systemic institutional racism being run in those institutions by the NCAA.

At the same time, according to the latest statistics available from a database kept by *USA Today*, between 2013 and 2017 there were 212 felony arrests of NFL players, 90 percent of which were black. As of September 2017, there had been 32 felony arrests of NFL players, and 97 percent of those were black.

These are nothing but bald, unbiased, cold, hard, statistical facts. Facts, though, when presented to the "we're all eeeeeeeeequal" nutcases, can result in thrown rocks and bottles.

Even at that risk, some more facts should be stated in brief.

Could Someone Please Notify the FBI and Census Bureau?

Neither the U.S. Federal Bureau of Investigation nor the U.S. Census Bureau have found out that race is just a "myth." The Census Bureau still has the population divided into five identified racial categories: White, Black or African American, American Indian or Alaska Native, Asian, and Native Hawaiian or Other Pacific Islander. It's a perfectly sensible organization of the understanding of the diversity of the human race and its cultures (well, except for some of the "experts" of academia and the United Nations), and the fact of such analysis gives people in those racial categories a chance to have a sense of belonging to, and a sense of pride in, the amazing array of creative and unique elements of the cultures arising from the races.

The FBI also has not gotten the memo—after 67 years. It hasn't figured out that it is merely living in some mythological fantasy world of faux "races," and so continues to keep very valuable statistics on crime, broken down into the races of those committing such crimes. The FBI statistics are publicly available. People who want to be honestly informed, and not trying to push some "equality" agenda, should look at them. Here, as more hard, cold fact is the FBI's overview of the 2016 statistics

In 2016, 69.6 percent of all individuals arrested were White, 26.9 percent were Black or African American, and 3.6 percent were of other races.

Of arrestees for whom ethnicity was reported, 18.4 percent were Hispanic.

Of all juveniles (persons under the age of 18) arrested in 2016, 62.1 percent were White, 34.7 percent were Black or African American, and 3.2 percent were of other races.

Of juvenile arrestees for whom ethnicity was reported, 22.8 percent were Hispanic.

Of all adults arrested in 2016, 70.2 percent were White, 26.2 percent were Black or African American, and 3.6 percent were of other races.

Of adult arrestees for whom ethnicity was reported, 18.0 were Hispanic.

White individuals were arrested more often for violent crimes than individuals of any other race and accounted for 59.0 percent of those arrests.

Of adults arrested for murder, 52.0 percent were Black or African American, 45.4 percent were White, and 2.6 percent were of other races.

Black or African American juveniles comprised 52.0 percent of all juveniles arrested for violent crimes. White juveniles accounted for 58.4 percent of all juveniles arrested for property crimes.

Of juveniles arrested for drug abuse violations, 74.8 percent were White.

White juveniles comprised 64.7 percent of juveniles arrested for rape and 60.2 percent of juveniles arrested for larceny-theft.

Well, there's a stunner for anybody thinking there was going to be some biased, racist slant against blacks or any other race. The entire point is that facts are facts are facts, and people only twist or misrepresent facts who are pushing some false agenda, not people who are interested in a dispassionate and rational discussion of facts.

And the facts, wherever you find them, prove conclusively that we are not all one giant homogenized lump of "equal" tar. If we were, I could sing "What'd I Say" or "America the Beautiful" every bit as soulfully and movingly as Ray Charles. I can't. Damn it. There are differences among the races, just as there are differences among people within races. If you don't believe it, take it up with the NFL and the NBA, not with me.

The Races Are Different

Is the Nobel Prize Committee "racist"? If not, how would you account for the fact that they never once have awarded a prize in the sciences of physics, chemistry, or medicine to a black person?

How about standard IQ tests? Are those "racist"? Let's turn to some vaunted and degreed "experts" on the subject. They must be good for something. No less a duo of august authorities than J. Philippe Rushton, Department of Psychology, The University of Western Ontario, London, Ontario, Canada, and Arthur R. Jensen, School of Education, University of California, Berkeley, published a paper entitled "Thirty Years of Research on Race Differences in Cognitive Ability," in the journal *Psychology, Public Policy, and Law,* 2005, Vol. 11, No. 2, 235–294. It carries a copyright of the American Psychological Association—and lord knows we'd never dare to question their authoritarian authoritarianism.

It's very long and scholarly and "experty," so I've donned my hip boots and waded out into the sucking tar pit for you—because I care about you—to drag back some of the relevant findings of 30 years of testing and retesting and retesting, fished out of the muck of about 30 tons of tarry reasons, reasons, reasons, reasons, reasons for the testing having refused to produce results that the "we're all eeeeeeequal" crowd want them to produce. Here are a few of the findings, below, and if you want more, you're just going to have to wade out into that tar on your own. (I suggest you get somebody to hold a rope tied around you.)

> [One] study also found that the average IQ for African Americans was lower than those for Latino, White, Asian, and Jewish Americans (85, 89, 103, 106, and 113, respectively; Herrnstein & Murray, 1994, pp. 273–278). ...
>
> [From another analysis] Around the world, the average IQ for East Asians centers around 106; that for Whites, about 100; and that for Blacks, about 85 in the United States and 70 in sub-Saharan Africa. ...
>
> On the Differential Aptitude Battery, by age 6, however, the average IQ of East Asian children is 107, compared with 103 for White children and 89 for Black children (Lynn, 1996). ...
>
> A study by Rushton (1997) analyzed recorded head circumference measurements and IQ scores from 50,000 children ... . Within each race, cranial capacity correlated with IQ scores. By age 7, the Asian American children averaged an IQ of 110; the White children, 102; and the Black children 90. Because the Asian American children were the shortest in stature and the lightest in weight while the Black children were the tallest in stature and the heaviest in weight, these average race differences in brain-size/IQ relations were not due to body size.
>
> [In another study] The 7-year-old White biological (i.e., nonadopted) children had an average IQ of 117 ... similar to that found for children of White upper-middle-class parents. The adopted children with two White biological parents had a mean IQ of 112. The adopted children with one Black and one White biological parent averaged 109. The adopted children with two Black biological parents had an average IQ of 97. (A mixed group of 21 Asian, North American Indian, and Latin American Indian adopted children averaged an IQ of 100 but were not included in the main statistical analyses.) ...
>
> [Same group, at age 17] The nonadopted White children had a mean IQ of 109 ... . The adopted children with two White biological parents had a mean IQ of 106 ... . The adopted children with one Black and one White biological parent had a mean IQ of 99 ... . The adopted children with two Black biological parents had a mean IQ of 89 ... .

And it just goes on and on and on and on, with one set of "experts" attacking another set of "experts" on their methodology, and another set of "experts" insisting that it's all environmental, and another set of "experts" insisting that it's all hereditary, and another set of "experts" saying that the tests are all slanted in some direction or another, and another set just chattering like baboons just for the sake of arguing and quoting other "experts" to prove that they're all experts.

And you know something that not a single one of these "experts" ever stops even to mention, or to think the thought, not even for one single word or moment?

They never *once* even consider that there is a hidden influence, another element, that is absolutely wreaking hell with their findings: that there is a *spiritual being* associated with and animating whatever *homo sapiens* body they have in front of them—no matter what color its skin is, no matter what color or texture its hair is, no matter what size its cranium is, and no matter what its athletic ability is.

Nope. These "experts" are hard-nosed materialists, just like John Locke, just like Charles Darwin, just like Julius Robert Oppenheimer, who helped Frankie the Limper Roosevelt create a weapon that would annihilate, incinerate, slaughter, and viciously mutilate tens of thousands of these *homo sapiens* bodies at a time.

They all consider that man is merely another animal. And because of that one fact, there is not one of these "experts" walking who has any slightest idea how to raise the IQ of any of them.

They never drop their pens or smart phones with a sudden realization that spiritual beings aren't any color or race at all.

So the entire merry-go-round-to-nowhere on "race" goes round, and round, and round, and ends up exactly nowhere.

The Races of Man Are Different. So What?

The question of "superiority vs. inferiority" among races is a specious and circular, tail-chasing, Smoking-Caterpillar, obscenely stupid waste of time. Had it not visited so much suffering and violence and injustice on so many decent and invaluable people in the world, of every race, the underlying question itself would be something about which to fall down on a patch of very unequal grasses and laugh yourself blue. Or green (new races).

There is no measuring stick for races. And worse, if there were, no one is qualified to hold it. The irony that the gibbering father of the entire absurd argument of "equality," John Locke, was a slave trader is not to laugh about, but to weep.

The race for "equality" among races is as infinitely circular as a race for "equality" among individuals, just on a grander scale. "Equality" at what? IQ tests? Football? Blues or gospel music? Sinking a three-pointer from center court, nothing but net? Inventing things in the technical sciences that advance the quality of life? Weaving intricate and beautiful baskets or rugs that enhance the quality of life? Just exactly what the *hell* are all the races supposed to be "equal" in?

How can there be a contest in which the goal is "equality"? There is no possible finish line for "equality." The race race cannot be won or lost. It just runs endlessly in tail-chasing circles. If any race "won" the race, then the race for equality would be lost! And if "equality" were achieved, there would be no more races discernible in mankind to continue to run the race race anyway.

So step off of hamster wheel that was John Locke's mind (a charitable expenditure of a noun), and cherish and value the unique and admirable qualities of every individual, every culture, every race, every group, every nation.

Culture is far more important than race. Some cultures are of one race because some races have within them many varied and wondrous cultures. Some cultures are mixtures of several or many races. Each culture has unique character and value that every other culture can benefit from, learn from, share and profit from.

If we cram all races together with ridiculous orders that, "You have to get along with each other, children, because you're all the same," there is always going to be friction—not to mention violation of the right of freedom of assembly.

One of the other wonderful propaganda campaigns being run all over the world right now is "interracial marriage." At last count, only about 3 percent of Americans were in an interracial relationship, but to turn on any television in America, you'd swear that it easily has to be 80 percent of the population. And just like with the merciless propaganda war against heterosexuals, this is an orchestrated propaganda war against *your* race—no matter what race you are. It is a knowing, intentional effort to eradicate the races, and turn everyone in the world into a homogenized undifferentiated animal. If you believe otherwise, I've got a bridge into a tar pit I'd like to sell you.

To hell with racial "equality." *Vive la difference!*

12. How Rights Go Wrong: Workplace Equality
Humanoid Resources

If you've been to any bank or financial institution, or if you've applied in person for credit on anything, or if you have been to any state or local or federal government office for any official document, license, or service, or if you have gone in person to order internet or TV or telephone service, or if you've attempted to travel on a train or plane, it's almost certain that you've been met with a demand like this from a "customer service" employee or a public "servant":

"I need to see your driver's license."

There can be a variation on such demands, such as "I need to see your I.D.," or "I need your Social Security number"—often without so much as a hint of a smile. My answer, invariably, to such rude arrogance is: "I'm not here to serve your needs. You're being paid to serve mine. So I need you to ask politely, courteously, in a warm and friendly manner, for anything of mine you'd like to see." That should be your answer, too. Invariably.

This haughty, imperious disdain for customers—and especially for citizens attempting to get service from their tax-supported bureaucratic "public servants"—is the zombie-world legacy of Lockean lunacy gone hog-wild in the workplace.

The mass hypnotic idiocy with which mankind has chased around for centuries on the snipe hunt dreamed up by John Locke for "equality" is inexhaustible, and perhaps is nowhere more pathetically laughable than in the workaday Western world.

If you sit down with any rational businessperson and ask exactly what is involved in trying to achieve "equality" in a group structure that cannot possibly be other than hierarchical, don't have any later appointments booked. This government-mandated Lockean lunacy isn't confined to commercial enterprises, though: it pervades every organized group of any description, every bureaucracy at every level of government, even the military.

No enterprise can launch itself into action anywhere, for any good and worthwhile purpose, without first passing the smell test for due regard to "equality." It is mandated mediocrity. It slows everything and everyone to a monitored crawl with spot checks for "equality." It has put insufferably supercilious asses on the "customer service" phones of every monopolistic utility that stands. It has flooded corporate cubicles with degreed magpies mouthing corporate-speak catch phrases to hide the fact that their expensive education didn't teach them anything they can use to get something actually and effectively done.

Nobody in governmental rubber-stamping cubicles gives a damn about effectiveness or worthiness of purpose, or for the vision of the creators of the group or activity to best know how to put it together and staff it and run it.

God forbid that any employer be *discriminate* in selecting help, because "discrimination" has been hijacked as a word and made into one of the filthiest, most damning wads of offal that can be thrown. It used to mean to make sensible decisions, to judge wisely, to perceive the distinguishing features of—all of which go hand in hand, inspection and discernment being required for sensible judgment and decision. Now the definition has been inverted to mean its opposite; now it means to make "distinctions" based on class or category or race or gender or perversity without regard to individual merit, which effectively has cancelled the word out of existence.

Another societal tidal wave of Lockeanism, largely influenced by disciples of Locke's disciple Wundt, has led to the meteoric rise of a "Department of Human Resources" in every major Western business. The name should be a source of shame for any government or business executive in the world who has it on the door of any office. It is utterly dehumanizing—which is what it was designed to be. It also is a misnomer. Its mission, in fact, is to know as little about what makes a particular "resource" a unique *human being* as possible. Otherwise, perception of distinguishing characteristics might lead someone to a fit of sound decision-making. Therefore the names on all relevant doors and desks should be changed to "Department of Humanoid Resources." (If this touches off a wave of vandalism, I'm very sorry. No, really.)

"Equality" in the workplace is a Lockean phantasm of uberequal man-animals.

The Only Real Dignity Possible in Any Workplace

There is one, and only one, way to allow people to find dignity in any workplace, whether its private, public, civil, educational, religious, or mystical: that's to recognize that every last job of any description that exists anywhere is vitally important, and that every last employee employed in any activity is a manager of a vital, indispensable function of the activity. If the job weren't valuable to somebody somewhere, it wouldn't exist.

Human beings are not machines, and they are not cogs in machines, but there is an applicable analogy in that every last cog, screw, spring, and gimmegahoojit (technical term) of any description in any machine is there to keep the machine running and producing whatever service or product that machine produces.

There are no "menial" jobs. That does not mean that "all jobs are equal." That's absurd. There must be executives who make tough decisions, and financial people who make tough decisions. In many industries and departments and divisions there must be middle managers and hiring specialists, and if all of the staff, whether one or 1,000, are not on a sensible hierarchical organizing system there will be chaos.

But no matter how extensive or complicated any such organizing system is, or how many people are involved, or how many layers of hierarchy there are, or how far down the totem pole anybody is, every last staff member is a vital, important part of that living group, and should be made aware of that fact constantly.

The constant striving for climbing some ladder or "breaking" some nonexistent "ceiling" all for status and competitiveness is a constantly destructive force in any organization. A reasonable system for people to be trained and apprenticed and move up is all well and good, but somebody who is masterful at putting widgets together should be able to be proud to spend his working hours putting widgets together at a reasonable wage and demonstrating his competence at putting the vital, indispensable widgets together.

Get Off of the Obsessive "Degree" Merry-Go-Round of Tar-Pitiness and Pettiness

I'm going to take the liberty—because I can—of speaking for a moment only anecdotally, because in my eclectic career I've had the honor of managing some departments and divisions in organizations, and some of the best and brightest people I ever had working with me had never seen the inside of a college or university. In fact, it was my personal observation and experience that some who had gotten a "degree" had their best accomplishments in spite of, not because of, any such education or "degree."

Look in any "help wanted" listing anywhere and you will be mowed down by demands for degrees, degrees, degrees, and more degrees, whether the job needs a damned "degree" or not. It is the "elitism" of the "experts" in our societies and cultures—such as some of the ones you met herein, who are so hyper-"educated" that they couldn't agree on whether the sun was up or down. But this educational elitism is every bit as haughty, supercilious, and holier-than-thou as any aristocracy that ever has existed.

The flabbergasting statistic that should strike terror into the hearts of anyone who actually cares about the United States and the well-being of its people is that only about a third of the population has a four-year-or-more degree—and an even more terrifying number of those can't find work, while being so buried in tarry debt from their pursuit of a "degree" that they may never be able to find out whether the sun is up or down. The percentage of "degreed" Americans has been driven up, up, up, up constantly since statistics are available, through a constant hammering of propaganda—pushed through tax-supported public schools—for the enrichment of the colleges and universities, and the student loan lenders. In 1940, only 5.5 percent of males and 3.8 percent of females had degrees. God only knows how America limped along at all.

The fact that ~33 percent of today's population has a four-year-or-better degree automatically *excludes* two-thirds of the population from employment in a huge percentage of available jobs, not because they are incompetent or stupid or lazy, but because they automatically get a big red REJECTED stamp on their applications by the Department of Humanoid Services when they don't have a degree.

People who aren't utilized in a society or culture are wasted by that society or culture, and far too many business owners and executives have fallen under the poisoned propaganda of the "experts" of academia—and, worse, the poisoned propaganda of the revoltingly greedy lenders of "student loans," who are binding our young people into unbreakable chains of debt slavery with the disgusting lie that they cannot succeed in life without paying dearly, direly, for a ticket on the merry-go-round to nowhere chasing a "degree."

And perhaps the saddest and most disgusting fact of all is that these "degree" factories are going around the clock, night and day, to ensure that every person they push out the door, burdened in crushing debt, is "equal" to all the rest.

Hire people. Look at them, talk to them, get to know them as human beings, not as another churned-out cookie-cutter created-equal "degree" bearer. Give them a chance. You may have to let some go, but you also may find some of the best employees you ever could hope for.

Bring Back Vocational Schools

Part of the university elitism has been to look down the academic noses at schools that train people not in "degrees," but in actually useful, productive skills and arts. These schools and institutions should be elevated in public perception to receive the respect they richly deserve. Any effort in the direction of making such training available and of interest to young people coming out of high school, and of creating more jobs where those arts and skills have value, could give an enormous boost to the morale, happiness, and sense of self worth of our next generations, and to an elevation of the civilization.

13. Of Despots and Depravity: Salvaging Human Rights
Suffer Not the Children to Go unto The Tar Pit of "Equality"

If "all men are created equal," then John Wayne Gacy is the poster boy for daycare keepers.

Adolf Eichmann is the standard of polished gentlemanly service to God and state.

The beet-red grocery cart pusher with swollen black feet and a garbage bag shirt is the archetype of attainment.

Typhoid Annie is your waitress.

If you recoil, you recoil not from the idiocy of extreme examples of the idea, but from the idiocy that is toxically inherent in the idea itself, since without that, no such extreme examples of toxic idiocy would be possible. The idiocy isn't resident in the examples; the examples are in exact compliance with the idea. The idiocy is resident, then, in the idea.

The idiot idea has been rampant in the world for centuries, held out to the world as a model of philosophical genius. But how else could it be, since if all are created equal, then the idiot is a genius, and so idiocy is genius.

Little despots, and the depraved, and the not-too-bright, and the unable *love* the idea, cling to the idea, praise the idea, feel threatened if the idea is questioned or challenged. It's how they are able to get into positions of power enough to drag everything and everybody within the reach of their stolen power down to their level. It's how the entire culture has been, and continues to be, dragged down toward a quagmire, a tar pit, of idiocy and depravity monitored by despotic and hate-filled little standing armies—whether in uniform or in gang colors.

It's how universities get filled with degreed oafs who will teach exactly such idiocy as though it were genius.

It's how education standards are whittled down daily toward the least "equal" of the "equal." The incredible dullness and monotony of it all renders the bright and able, in their restlessness, candidates for the Wundtian despot down the hall, who is ready to dole out pills to bring them down closer to this week's acceptable standard of "equal." Educators: if you have a real interest in the future of the students at heart, and have not become enslaved to the "equality" herding, demand that your educational institutions throw out this horse-and-buggy system of "grade years" education that drags every student down into the tar. Bring education into the 21st century, where students enrolled in a program of study for any milestone go *at their own pace* through a checklist of materials and intended accomplishments in application. Don't "teach at" them; guide them with encouragement and help to accomplish their study goals—but not in an environment that smacks of "competition" with other students, or a race against the calendar.

There are modern systems of education and training available that address all the pitfalls of study for any student, in any subject, so that all can progress and learn at their own pace. Find them and demand that they be implemented.

What Rights Are Right?

I'm going to revisit, only for a moment, the amazingly destructive primary premise of the *Universal Declaration of Human Rights* being foisted off on the world by the United Nations:

> All human beings are born free and equal in dignity and rights.

That is in the running for the single most deadly poisonous and evil dogma ever shoved down the throat of humankind.

Not only are useful standards of excellence and accomplishment and refinement practically eradicated from civilization and culture by such insanity, any thought of such standards is actively discouraged as being somehow "discriminatory," or not politically correct, or somehow demeaning to some "equal" who has a divine "right" to feel "equalized" instead of challenged to achieve or aspire.

Dignity and respect are earned, not owed as a birthright. Richard J. Herrnstein and Charles Murray, in their seminal work *The Bell Curve* make the compelling and sensible case on the subject of human dignity:

> The central measure of success for this government, as for any other, is to permit people to live lives of dignity—not to give them dignity, for that is not in any government's power, but to make it accessible to all. That is one way of thinking about what the Founders had in mind when they proclaimed, as a truth self-evident, that all men are created equal. That is what we have in mind when we talk about valued places for everyone.
>
> Inequality of endowments, including intelligence, is a reality. Trying to pretend that inequality does not really exist has led to disaster. Trying to eradicate inequality with artificially manufactured outcomes has led to disaster. It is time for America once again to try living with inequality, as life is lived: understanding that each human being has strengths and weaknesses, qualities we admire and qualities we do not admire, competencies and incompetences, assets and debits; that the success of each human life is not measured externally but internally; that of all the rewards we can confer on each other, the most precious is a place as a valued fellow citizen.

That rational approach allows for each to contribute to a society and a culture those talents, skills, abilities, and competencies of which he is endowed, without being held to some false and foolish "standard" that doesn't exist, striving for the impossible Lockean delusion of "equality."

Until all such Lockean poison is flushed from a culture's system, it is a culture and a civilization that is dying a long, slow, agonizing death of systemic poisoning.

It is inarguable that all beings in this world have certain rights. That isn't contested at all.

Certainly all human beings have rights to their own lives, rights to express themselves freely, rights to defend themselves, rights to procreate for the future of mankind, and rights to worship any faith or god they choose.

The key part of the equation that was entirely omitted by Locke, Jefferson, and the United Nations is that no such "rights" can possibly survive amongst mankind without equivalent *responsibility* and *accountability* in the exercise of such rights. That includes honesty and trust.

Rights are destroyed by dishonesty, lies, deceit, and duplicity used to accomplish the 180-degree opposite of human rights—but in the name of having "rights." So it is terribly irresponsible to issue any declaration or list of "rights" without a balancing list of responsibilities that accompany such rights.

If all men have rights to their own lives, then all men have the responsibility not to destroy the lives of others.

If all men have the right to express themselves freely, then all men have the responsibility to allow others to express themselves freely.

If all men have the right to procreate for the future of mankind, then all men have the responsibility to support and protect procreation for the survival of the human race.

If all men have the right to defend themselves, then all men have the responsibility to support and protect the right to adequate self-defense.

If all men have the right to worship any faith or god they choose, then all men have the responsibility to preserve and defend the sanctity and safety of the religions and faiths of others.

Other rights—and concomitant responsibilities—might well be listed by men of good faith, but it is pointless and dictatorial to issue an arbitrary list of purported "rights," as the United Nations did, when there is no firm and self-determined *agreement* on such rights—and equivalent responsibilities—by the group of individuals being subjected to the enforcement of such alleged "rights." Without broad agreement, and a harmonious shared purpose to bring about the realization of such rights—and responsibilities—issuing decrees of "rights" is merely adding more tar to the tar pit.

A Farewell and Thank You to John Locke

On the basis that even a broken clock is right twice a day, John Locke certainly got one thing right in his often tortured days and nights of wrestling with his demons:

> Men take up prejudice to truth without being aware of it, and afterwards feed only on those things that suit with and increase the vicious humour.

The world has fed too long on that which suits with and increases the "vicious humour" arising from the nightmare world in which "all men are created equal." It is tar.

Only when we each, and all together, begin to fully recognize and fully appreciate the uniqueness of every one of us will there ever be a chance for peace on Earth. And I wish you just such peace.

Afterword: Equality Realized?
The Homogeneous Culture Curdles

The Lockean universe populated by men all "created equal" has been the stuff of horror stories since the genre was invented, not by Mary Shelley but around primitive campfires. It's older than the Hebrew golem—outwardly a real person but lacking the human dimension of personality. It lay in the vampire legends, it populated Metropolis, it arrived in pod trucks in *Invasion of the Body Snatchers,* and is in every zombie movie ever made. Orwell warned us against it in his book *1984,* but he was over a century too late.

John Locke, the frail and pale little golem, had already come and deposited his seed to create a world of "created equal" golems.

How homogeneous is "equal" enough?

Would the materialists and their cheap lounge-lizard parlor magician and their pill pushers in every school celebrate if they could snuff out the last flame of hope anywhere in the world that there is something in man that transcends the matter of stones?

Will the crusaders for "racial equality" feel fulfilled when there is only one perfectly blended and indistinguishable race? Would "race" have any meaning or value left at all?

Will the anti-genderists breathe easy when no uniquely feminine or masculine quality is left in evidence, in a world of perfect hermaphrodites—or neuters?

Will the leaders of Islam never face and acknowledge the fact that there are seeds of oppression, destruction, slaughter buried in its dogma that make it deadly to the rights and freedoms of its fellow man?

Will America not lay down its arms and standing armies until every citizen is in compliant sameness, and every nation in the world its own national clone?

Is the materialistic quest for living clones going to be enough "equality" to satiate the hunger for sameness? If the quest for "equality" is ever realized anywhere, in any quarter, what is its reward besides a living Hell of infinite unrelieved monotony?

There was a truly great philosopher from the 20th century, who by all indications was assassinated in 1972 in a coordinated operation of the CIA, the Five Eyes, and Hassan II of Morocco. I learned much about his philosophy in researching my book *Watergate: The Hoax*, where that convoluted story is told, and I owe him a debt for some of the concepts spoken of in this book. He has had his name and reputation and benign philosophy smeared through the tar and mud for decades by the very organizations who murdered him and their Operation Mockingbird media mouthpieces, but he left words that all mankind would do well to heed:

> When the fires of ideology threaten to consume us all, it is time to forget politics and seek reason. —**L. Ron Hubbard**, *The Fundamental of Thought*

It has never been truer that it is time to forget politics and seek reason. While our similarities bind us together, only our differences make us each unique, and it's the sharing and exchanging of our unique qualities and creations that make life interesting enough to live. None of us must lose sight of our similarities, but if man is to move his cultures away from barbaric wars, up from degraded mediocrity, out toward the stars, forward to new and fresh and vibrant ideas, he first must escape from the tar pit of "equality."

Created equal?

It's the greatest lie ever told.

About the Author

Ashton Gray lives somewhere in the South, and that's about all he would care to say. He was interviewed on Coast to Coast A.M. after the release of his landmark 600-page exposé, *Watergate: The Hoax,* and has been interviewed for an upcoming documentary film covering many of the issues raised in that book. Currently he is hard at work on its sequel, *Stargate: The Hoax,* scheduled for a release likely in late 2018.

Visit us online:

CHALET BOOKS & MULTIMEDIA
www.chaletbooks.com

OMEN BOOKS
www.omenbooks.com

www.ingramcontent.com/pod-product-compliance
Lightning Source LLC
LaVergne TN
LVHW051630080426
835511LV00016B/2276